JANINE ASSA

Translated by Anne Hollander

The Great
Roman Ladies

Evergreen Profile Book 13

GROVE PRESS, INC. NEW YORK
EVERGREEN BOOKS LTD. LONDON

FIRST PUBLISHED IN THIS EDITION 1960. ALL RIGHTS RESERVED.

Library of Congress Catalog Card Number: 59-10790

Evergreen Profile Books are published

in the United States by Grove Press, Inc.

64 University Place   New York 3, N.Y.

in Great Britain by Evergreen Books Ltd.

17 Sackville Street   London, W. 1

Distributed in Canada by McClelland & Stewart Ltd., 25 Hollinger Rd., Toronto 16

First published in France by Editions du Seuil, Paris,

as Les Grandes Dames Romaines

MANUFACTURED BY MOUTON & CO., IN THE NETHERLANDS

The Great Roman Ladies
by Janine Assa

Contents

Introduction

Half the human race – and even a little more – is made up of women. This mathematical truth, which history occasionally overlooks, tends too often to take on the glamor of a modern discovery, of an achievement of contemporary scientific progress. Must we suppose that the creature born of Adam's rib has required so many centuries to reach 'perfection'? It can indeed be asserted that ever since antiquity – and even before the birth of the Roman Empire – our masculine forbears have had to deal with woman already in possession of all the qualities recognized in the sex, of which either amiability or weakness is generally emphasized, according to the desire to win women over or to rule them.

The early days of the Roman Empire are well known. They have often been retraced and described through the men who created that empire. Historians and psychologists have patiently taken apart the mechanism that allowed Augustus and his successors to establish a despotic regime in spite of the Roman repugnance for personal power. This mechanism, often used with great success since then, is relatively simple. It consists in safeguarding republican appearances. Without a doubt, speeches that celebrate liberty and democracy are less important than the institutions that ensure them, and have no other purpose than to lull the citizens to sleep and to benumb their alertness. At any rate, these speeches tend to arrest change and prevent revolution. Ancient and modern scholars have analyzed at length the original political system which was born with this period: from Augustus to Nero, through Tiberius, Caligula and Claudius

– the first imperial dynasty – the emperors of the Julio-Claudian family are familiar to us.

Even though Tacitus often favors women and certain satirists make a place for them which, while less distinguished is more considerable, the role of women in this history is both less prominent and less well examined. Why this omission?

Indeed, the Greek tradition was scarcely interested in women. In fact, it preserves only Aspasia's name. She was the daughter of a Milesian established in Athens, and consequently an alien. She was endowed with every charm, including those of intellect; she understood sophistry and rhetoric, and she was considered well informed in political matters. Pericles cast off his wife in order to set her up in his house, and imposed her, not without difficulty, on Athens. Actually, she was outside society – a hetaera, a courtesan, not a good woman. And this story, in which Pericles abandons his haughty reserve, illustrates the Greek conception of women: 'There are three kinds of women: hetaere to delight the soul, prostitutes to satisfy the senses, and respectable women to bear children and keep house.'

This definition makes it easy to understand why the Athenian woman only appears in a domestic capacity, or in literary portraits which dwell on her innocence and simplicity or on her shrewishness. The ideal was to allow her 'to see and hear as few things as possible before marriage' so as to 'have her spoken of as little as possible whether favorably or unfavorably.' Brought up in the part of the house set aside for women, the gynecium, she dedicated her dolls in the temple of Artemis at the time of her marriage, between the ages of twelve and fifteen. Her husband, who was about thirty, finished her education. Here is the advice given to the bride by Xenophon in the *Economics*:

> You will have to remain at home, to make those servants go out together who work outdoors, and oversee those who work in the house; you will have to receive the provisions which are brought, distribute those which are to be used, keeping those which must be saved, seeing to it that the reserves of a year are not used up in a month. When wool is brought to you, you should see that garments are woven of it for those who need them, and see also that the supplies remain good ... if one of the servants falls ill, you will devote all your efforts to curing him.

There are exceptions to this classic portrait. Certain poets and philosophers placed married couples on an equal footing and wished to give women an education. Mainly, there was the case of the Spartan woman, whom Greece freely mocked. In Sparta the worlds of the sexes were so divided that women acquired real independence. The young girl went to exercise in the stadium and became hardened to fatigue. The freedom of her dress, with 'bare thighs, floating tunic,' seemed intolerable to the Athenians. Once married, the young woman – whose mission was to give birth to fine warriors – in fact ruled the house. The man, taken up with military obligations, was never there. Financial dealings were forbidden to Spartan citizens, and it was the women who managed the property and handled the funds. Their free habits, their maternal pride, and their financial power were the scandal of Greece.

Originally the Roman woman was nothing in her own right. An eternal minor, she passed from the guardianship of her father

Bare thighs, floating tunic.   *Innocence and simplicity.*

to that of her husband. But from the beginning of Roman history she appears very different from the Greek woman. The Roman lady ran the house and thus acquired an undeniable authority. Pejorative in French, the term *matrona* in Latin indicates the woman of quality, with a nuance of respectability, virtue, and likewise authority. If classic Greek history preserves only Aspasia's name, republican Roman history preserves virtuous or heroic women from Lucretia to Cornelia, the mother of the Gracchi. In addition, custom was to take the place of law: the end of the republic became a period of feminine emancipation. The law then came to the rescue, and woman gradually was freed of all guardianship.

Certain women stand out in Roman republican history, but those of the empire and particularly those of the imperial family take on a singular prominence. These 'ladies of the family' play the starring roles in this book; but the secondary characters only seem to suffer – they have not been forgotten. They followed the fashion in dress, thought, and action and the fashion was set by the princesses. To speak of these latter, to follow in their sovereign footsteps, is also to render tacit homage to all their imitators – to the senator's wife who did her hair like Julia's, the banker's wife who was as extravagant as Poppaea, the governor's wife who, in the obscurity of her far-off province, behaved like Messalina . . .

Women played so much greater a part in the imperial family because they transmitted the dynastic line. When a man arrives at absolute power under whatever title – king, emperor, or dictator – anxiety about handing on his work soon haunts him. He needs a male heir. Bonaparte, once he became Napoleon, felt this need for a son to the extent of divorcing his wife for reasons of state in order to find a woman capable of providing one. It is certain that the life of a dynasty is less difficult when the succession poses no problems. When one thinks of the history of French royalty and the formation of the French kingdom, the slow but sure increase of power and territory which continued throughout the centuries, one realizes that the Capetian kings were always lucky enough to have direct heirs. On the day the three sons of Philip the Fair disappeared, leaving only daughters, a serious crisis of succession began: the Hundred Years' War. But French royalty was already firm enough to withstand so violent a storm.

The history of the first dynasty of Roman emperors, on the

other hand, is that of a family without male heirs. Nevertheless, they stubbornly tried to remain a family; and concern about the bloodline, usually quite foreign to Romans, preoccupied the sovereigns.

The first of the celebrated men in the family contains within himself the defects and the difficulties of his descendants. Everyone knows him – Julius Caesar. In the course of the funeral oration which he delivered in 68 B.C. for his aunt Julia, he claimed that the *gens Julia* had existed since the foundation of Rome and was descended from the goddess Venus. Although married five times to women of noble birth, and in spite of his reputation among the soldiers, Caesar had but one child, Julia, a much-loved daughter. He married her to Pompey the Great, and she gave birth to a son; but she soon died, and her son did not survive her. Julius Caesar then had no direct descendants.

Nevertheless, the entire family was ostentatiously to claim relationship with 'the divine Julius,' and this ancestry was not to be as fantastic as the connection between Aunt Julia and Venus. The blood tie with the 'bald, epileptic seducer,' prized by all who succeeded him – since Caesar's glory increased after his death – was transmitted through women.

Caesar had a sister, married to Attius Balbus, who brought a daughter into the world. The latter had two daughters and a son, Octavius. This grandnephew of Caesar became his legal son by adoption. There had always existed in Rome a custom which allowed great families, threatened with extinction for lack of male descendants, to 'buy a son,' usually of another great family. This custom was originally explained by religious reasons: the ancestral cult of the *gens* was thus perpetuated.

From Augustus to Nero the same process appears: the head of the state would have no son (Augustus, Caligula, Nero) or perhaps the son would die before his father (Tiberius) or he would be too young (Claudius); the emperor adopted one or several young men capable of succeeding him, and adoption marked them out for the empire. In any case, each reign posed its problems and solved them according to the order of masculine decease and the sentimental intrigues of the women.

The success of the founder of the empire, Augustus, was incomplete for lack of a satisfactory solution to the problem of succession. His matrimonial adventures threw a series of women and their offspring into competition. After a broken engagement, Augustus first married Scribonia. By her he had a daughter,

Julia. But he set aside his wife on the pretext of immorality in order to steal Livia from her husband under rather unusual circumstances. This young woman was in fact the mother of a three-year-old boy, Tiberius, and she was expecting another child, which was born in Augustus' house three months after the remarriage. This was Drusus. But this lightning-bolt marriage was sterile. Here we have the heart of the imperial drama: from the rejected wife Scribonia, who survived Augustus, the entire family was to descend through Julia, while Livia, the beloved, respected, and honored wife was to be devoured with ambition for her own sons and desolate at not bearing a third child.

Two women already challenged each other on behalf of their offspring: Scribonia and Livia. It would seem to have been easy to solve everything by having Julia marry one of Livia's sons; in this way the union between the two female branches of the family would have produced the second generation. But here another consideration intervened. Augustus had a sister, Octavia, and her son Marcellus was also a scion of the blood of Caesar – the Emperor's sister's children should take precedence over those of his wife. So the imperial family from Augustus on was divided into three rival parties: Scribonia, Livia, Octavia – the rejected but fertile wife, the sterile wife, and the Emperor's sister.

The imperial continuity was transferred from one to the other of these feminine branches, each particular solution preceded by several tentative ones. Attempts and solutions both gave rise to the development of fierce hatred. Indeed, to familial and dynastic force was added the ambition and often the intelligence of some of these women. Faced with the power they sought during their lives, they often reacted violently and gave proof of a real thirst for domination: by their own will and thanks to circumstances favorable to them, women were bound up with the history of the empire. And so it is possible to trace this history from an almost exclusively feminine point of view. Two great ladies illustrate the imperial evolution as well as, if not better than, the five men who in turn occupied the highest office. The first, Livia, symbolizes the difficulties of a regime which is being built up; her prudence and diplomacy, her hidden influence which continued to assert itself, faithfully reflect the beginnings of the empire. Her power spread over half a century, extending well beyond Augustus' lifetime and continuing until

11

The "divine" Julius.

the Empress' death during the reign of her son Tiberius. One might speak of a 'reign of Livia.' Twenty years later, a woman once more took the title of 'the August.' She enthroned herself on a dais beside her husband, received embassies, ruled her son: this was the Empress Agrippina. She confirmed the omnipotence of imperial authority; the habit was formed and no excess would shake it. But Agrippina also symbolizes the new character assumed by the regime: though the institution was enduring, the lives of those who represented it were frail. Augustus and Livia died of old age, surrounded by universal respect; Agrippina, her brother Caligula, her husband Claudius, and her son Nero were all assassinated.

The Family

'Drinking, eating, sleeping together – this is marriage, so I gather.' The three ancient forms of marriage, *usus, confarreatio,* and *coemptio* – or cohabitation, ritual repast, and symbolic sale – combined to place a woman in marital tutelage, or rather to transfer her from the guardianship of the paterfamilias to that of the husband. Certain traditionalist families continued to remain attached to them for several generations, but in general practice all that fell into disuse.

Under the empire the marriage ceremony already resembled ours; it consisted of an exchange of consent. But it was not a public function. Neither the state nor the religion of the city intervened. Though the ceremony was purely private, some enjoyed embellishing it with intricacies: a religious ritual or an official escorting of the young bride to her husband's house had no other function than to make a matter-of-fact situation more solemn.

In such a marriage, as we shall see, the woman did not completely come under her husband's control, but sometimes remained legally in the bosom of her original family. It became necessary for legislation to establish the existence of reciprocal obligations between married people, and between a mother and her children.

In other cases too, the state concerned itself with marital relations: Augustus promulgated a law concerning adultery. For sixty days the father or the husband enjoyed the exclusive right to punish the guilty wife, but after this interval the right belonged to anyone. What was more, the husband could not pardon; he was bound to repudiate the adulterous wife.

15

Marriage was preceded by betrothal. The age varied a great deal, and sentiment was very often excluded. The custom scarcely differed from the practice dear to the *ancien régime* or to Oriental peoples: agreement between the two families constituted all that was essential; young girls were betrothed while they were still children. Tiberius' first wife, Vipsania Agrippina, one of Agrippa's daughters, was engaged at the age of one year; Octavia, the daughter of Claudius and Messalina, was seven years old when she was betrothed to Nero.

The betrothal ceremony was not so solemn as that of marriage. It consisted basically of a banquet where relatives and friends gathered as witnesses to the concluded agreement. The young man had to offer the girl gifts, of which the principal one was a symbolic ring, a simple iron band sometimes encircled with gold, the pledge of fidelity which the future wife had to wear on the finger we now call the ring finger. The Romans had chosen this finger in preference to others because ancient science believed to have discovered in it a nerve communicating directly with the heart.

After the young girl had reached the legal marriageable age, in her twelfth year, the marriage ceremony took place. A girl was married between the ages of twelve and nineteen, the optimal age being between fourteen and sixteen. Agrippina the Younger

The marriage celebration.

married Domitius Ahenobarbus, her first husband, quite early, at the age of twelve; Livia was first married at sixteen; Julia began her series of marriages at fourteen ... At twenty a single Roman lady was already an old maid, subject to the penalty of the law against celibacy.

With the approach of the wedding, everyone was occupied exclusively in making up the young bride's trousseau, buying her jewels and finery, choosing the servants destined to follow her to her new home. When the great day arrived, the two dwellings of the engaged couple, resplendently draped with tapestries and garlands, were filled from daybreak on with relatives, friends, and hangers-on. The bride wore a tunic without a hem, drawn in with a woolen girdle and covered with a saffron-yellow mantle. A flame-colored veil covered her head, surmounted by a simple crown of field flowers. In her father's house, surrounded by her kin, she received her fiancé who was accompanied by his family and friends. A sacrifice, usually performed in the brilliantly lit and decorated atrium in the presence of ten witnesses, preceded the exchange of vows: *ubi tu Gaius ego Gaia* (where and when you will be Gaius, I shall be Gaia). The cheers and good wishes of the guests punctuated the ceremony, which became a prolonged and luxurious feast, the excess of which Augustus attempted to moderate by law. The total expense of a nuptial feast was not to exceed a thousand sesterces. This provision shared the fate of all overly ambitious laws: a thousand sesterces for

Dressing the bride.

the expenses of a festival plus gifts to the crowd and hangers-on!
The extreme modesty of the legal maximum condemned this law
to such rapid disuse that one wonders if it was ever applied at all.

When evening came, the newly married girl was conducted
to her husband's house: a noisy procession, preceded by flute-
players and torchbearers whose liveliness gave pleasure to neigh-
bors and passers-by.

By the light of the nuptial torch held aloft by the *pronubus,*
two other 'ushers' lifted the bride and carried her, her feet never
touching the ground, across the threshold of her married home,
which was decked with white draperies and garlands. The first
'bridesmaid' then led her to the nuptial chamber to which her
husband came, while the guests retired.

On leaving her father's household for her husband's, the young
married woman was furnished with an imposing trousseau, accompanied by plenty of servants, and became the possessor of
various property both personal and real, besides her dowry. In
the marriage of consent which became the ordinary form of

conjugal union, only the dowry became part of the husband's fortune; already the latter's rights had become severely restricted. This sheds light on the reaction Horace ascribes to the woman surprised *in flagrante delicto:* she fears for her dowry. All the wife's own property remained in her sole possesion; the husband did not even have a life interest in it. This property was inalienable and not distrainable even in the event of fraudulent bankruptcy. When the marriage was sincere and close, a husband might place the remainder of his own fortune in his wife's name before being declared insolvent, suspending his payments, and thus rendering himself inaccessible to the demands of his creditors. The edicts of Augustus and Claudius even forbade the wife to put up bail for her husband, so careful always was the law to protect feminine weakness which, for all it was affirmed, was not actually a reality.

The woman endowed with a judicious mind who had freed herself from paternal control, perhaps by means of emancipation, and whom marriage had not subjected to a husband's mastery, was then the administrator of all her possessions. She might manage them, draw up contracts, acquire and dispose of property, all with the co-operation of a guardian; but in practice this guardianship was not a burden, and she was easily free of it.

The unrestricted handling of her property gave her considerable independence, and among writers the rich woman was an ideal subject for satire. 'A woman thinks that everything is permitted her, she blushes at nothing any more, once she wears an emerald necklace and great pearls hang from her ears. Nothing is more intolerable than a rich woman.' In many cases the husband himself had nothing to say:

How can it be that even by her husband's showing, Cesennia is the best of wives? She brought him a thousand sesterces! He is paid to call her chaste. It is not with Venus' quiver that he grows thin or with her torch he burns; it is . . . from her dowry that the arrows come. She has bought her liberty: therefore, even in her husband's presence she may exchange signals, and answer her love-letters. A rich wife, with a covetous husband, has all a widow's privileges.

And so we have come to the purely formal marriages between rich women and poor men, which permitted both of them to evade the law against celibacy and allowed complete freedom to

19

each. Martial has the last word: 'You ask me why I don't want to marry a rich woman? Because I have no desire to become the humble servant of my own wife!'

For women, entering into marriage generally constituted an abrupt leap into independence, a sudden apprenticeship in freedom. All at once they became acquainted with a world which they might have glimpsed before but in which on principle they had had no share. An infinite variety of pleasures was offered them. Nothing in their education protected them against the temptations and dangers of society: the principal victim of these dangers would be the marriage itself.

Latin moralists and satirists of the first two centuries took pleasure in deploring Roman matrimonial habits, for which they very often held the women responsible. According to Juvenal, certain ladies counted years not by consuls but by husbands! Marriage and divorce seemed at that time an inevitable association. One married often, no matter how, because one could be divorced just as easily. There were many reasons for the dissolution of a marriage. Leaving death aside, the loss of liberty or of freedom of the city by one partner authorized the other to consider the marriage tie broken. Certain obstacles produced the same effect: a father-in-law who adopted his son-in-law without having taken the precaution of emancipating his daughter destroyed the marriage of his children. As for divorce, the procedure was the simplest possible: all that was necessary to put it into effect was a separation accompanied by an unequivocal manifestation of will.

This frequency of separations and remarriages corresponded to a general frame of mind at the end of the republic, which considered it proper that the union have a political or financial purpose. If the political situation changed, if the fortune collapsed, one broke the conjugal bond.

The imperial family, of course, followed and even speeded up this trend of the period. Political reasons here were fundamental, but they were incompatible with the desire expressed by Augustus to purify morals and strengthen the marriage tie. The facility with which Augustus married off members of his family, and had them divorced in order to remarry them elsewhere, as circumstances indicated, gives the lie to his moralistic pretensions.

The marital history of Augustus' only daughter is quite characteristic. But if Julia played a particularly important role from

20

the dynastic point of view, she is still only one example: almost all family marriages were accomplished the same way. We may pass over the broken engagements with two or three youths, of which one was no less than a son of Mark Antony, at the time of the triumvirate. Julia was still very young.

These attempts came to nothing. Childhood engagements were, as we know, a common thing under the republic, and so was the breaking of them. In great families the children were promised from birth. Augustus intervened to limit this increasing betrothal fever, by the use of certain population laws of fiscal basis, put into effect throughout his reign. From then on, one could no longer become engaged to a young girl before she reached the age of ten, and the marriage was to occur two years later at the legal age of nubility for Roman women.

Julia's first marriage seemed perfect. In the family there was a descendant of Caesar, the only son of Augustus' sister Octavia. He was named Marcellus. Having scarcely reached puberty, the texts state, Marcellus married Julia. They were seventeen and fourteen, respectively. An interesting point of etiquette: Augustus, the bride's father, was absent from Rome at the time of the wedding, and Agrippa, his chief associate, received the order to celebrate the marriage. Having been the recipient of many honors out of proportion to his years, designating him as Augustus' future successor, Marcellus fell ill two years later and died. At sixteen Julia was a childless widow, and there was no man left of Caesar's line. Augustus' successor thenceforth could only be Julia's son begotten by someone foreign to the blood of Venus Genetrix.

Who would be the father of Augustus' grandchildren? An important question. It had to be a man sufficiently remarkable to permit himself to be effaced by his sons, and yet who would please the Romans by his valor and rank so that he might be in a position to replace Augustus if necessary. For two years the Emperor searched, hesitated, waited. One is well aware, from the way in which ancient authors constructed their sentences, that after Marcellus' death he could not rest until Julia was married. The solution came from his near relatives. According to certain people, it was Octavia, Marcellus' own mother, who presented a proposition to him which seems extraordinary to us, but which faithfully reflects the habits of the epoch. She advised him to marry Julia to the man who for years had aided and seconded Augustus in everything, the one who won his battles and administered his territories. This methodical man of war, this devoted friend, this brilliant second-in-command was named Agrippa. His birth was obscure, but his position as Augustus' right hand had made him greatest after the Emperor. At forty-two, Agrippa was already married for the second time, to one of Octavia's daughters, Marcella, who had made him the father of several children. This illustrious marriage, by the way, proves the esteem and friendship in which he was held by the members of the imperial family. But Octavia proposed that Augustus have Agrippa divorce her daughter Marcella, so that he might marry her ex-daughter-in-law, Julia. And so Julia at eighteen was married again, this time to a man who could have been her father . . . .

This was not the only couple to be separated for Julia's sake: Agrippa died before Augustus, and Julia was a widow once more, but now with five children of whom two sons were adopted by her father. Was he going to marry her off again, and if so, how? Augustus expected much and made inquiries on all sides, even in the far-removed sphere of politics. Then a woman gained her object – Livia, who succeeded in getting Tiberius married to Julia. This, too, was a political marriage celebrated at the expense of feeling; Tiberius, in fact, had to divorce a dearly beloved wife, Vipsania Agrippina, herself the daughter of Agrippa's first marriage. She was already a mother and expecting another child. When Tiberius saw her a year later, he was so upset that it was arranged for him never to meet her again.

That was how this heiress found the necessary husbands: the man whose circumstances seemed suitable became hers, whatever the cost. As for her own reactions in regard to her different marriages, they also were characteristic of the time. Marriage was to confer upon her the position of first lady in the empire after Livia; and she would find elsewhere the emotional compensations to which she felt herself entitled.

This story shows us the chief criteria for marriage in the classic period among great families: political considerations were essential, sometimes based on birth, but most often on the necessities of the moment. In the most important cases, there was no hesitation in overriding religious or civil regulations. And so at the time of her union with Antony, Octavia had been the widow of her first husband for less than the ten months' legal interval before remarriage. For Julia's sake, wives were repudiated one after the other, some with children and one even pregnant, all of which was of no consequence. Livia, indeed, married Augustus three months before the birth of her second child, Drusus. Born in Augustus' house, the infant was then taken to the home of his legal father. The College of Priests had been consulted about the possibility of such a marriage. Two generations later, another infraction: marriage between uncle and niece, when Claudius married Agrippina the Younger. The senators had been bribed to pass a law authorizing this kind of union, considered incestuous until then. It was a question of a decree carried in the interests of state. The other citizens could then in their turn marry under these conditions. Once more the imperial family set the tone, since Agrippina, the great-granddaughter of Augustus and Livia, consumed with ambition, had succeeded in seducing her uncle Claudius as soon as he became emperor.

This last example is an exaggerated illustration of one of the most constant rules of marriage in the imperial family and in all great families: alliances within the family. With jealous care, Augustus made maximum use of Livia's and Octavia's children and grandchildren. Marriages between cousins, between children with one parent in common, all combinations were possible, so that in the third generations the ties were double, if not triple; and all the men ended by descending from all three – Augustus, Octavia, and Livia. The mental and physical defects thus accumulated explain the madness of a Caligula, the perversion of a Claudius, the monstrousness of a Nero.

Although the men always managed to marry in the family, once or several times, it was not the same for the women; and the choice of a husband outside the family posed a great problem. Perhaps the bridegroom-elect might belong to one of Rome's great families: the Aemilii, the Domitii, the Antonii; but then it was difficult to judge in advance his possible intentions. Distrust would be great on the part of the reigning emperor, and accusers would have a chance to denounce the true or false aims of these 'descendants' of Augustus, who would often suffer premature death. Or perhaps husbands of obscure origins might be chosen expressly in order to avoid all possible ambitions. That was how Tiberius married off his granddaughters. It nonetheless remains true that, for the ambitious, marriage seemed to suffice and could have sufficed. Thus Sejanus thought he could acquire a right to the empire by marrying Livilla, a young woman of the highest lineage, granddaughter of Octavia and Livia. The intrigue was so complex that it seems like fiction. While Livilla was the wife of Drusus, Tiberius' son, Sejanus undertook to seduce her; then he drove her to murder Drusus. Finally he asked Tiberius for her hand. The Emperor's answer is significant: personally, Tiberius had no objections to this union, but Livilla's rank risked tempting her husband to make rash claims. Another example, also rather unusual, was that of C. Silius, Messalina's 'forced' lover. The Empress did not hide her adultery. Quite the contrary, she gave it actual publicity, to the great discomfiture of Silius. To save his life, Silius proposed to marry the Empress and do away with Claudius. The change of husbands would involve, to his advantage, a change of emperors. Messalina's reaction is as significant as that of Tiberius: at first she received the idea coldly, afraid that once the deed was done, Silius would remember only the heinous crime. Nevertheless, she married him, and Claudius felt his throne threatened when he heard the news.

The results of such marriages are manifold and various. Instability of the union seemed the rule. One married twice or three times at least, divorced easily; and for a young woman to maintain widowhood after one marriage was almost shocking. Besides, the law obliged her to remarry.

Happy marriages appear extraordinary; they are cited as examples. One must set Livia and Augustus apart: for these two political creatures, interest demanded that they carry through an apparently close and successful union. Their conjugal life, with all its reciprocal concessions, seemed a triumph of will and of Livia's pliability. Faced with her husband's ardent temperament, she did not hesitate to close her eyes to numerous escapades: even more, she occasionally favored them. It was whispered that she caused certain closed litters to be led to her husband. She even tolerated the rivalry of Maecenas' wife Terentia, actually the official mistress. Augustus was madly infatuated with Terentia, to the point of undertaking a journey to Spain with her to prevent their liaison from causing too much gossip in Rome. But as a reward for her complaisance, Livia acquired and retained Augustus' respect. The words he spoke on his deathbed, in his wife's arms ('Remember our union, Livia'), bear witness to the solidity of this marriage.

Two couples appear truly happy, if not for long: Antonia the Younger and Drusus, son of Livia; and Agrippina the Elder and Germanicus. Evidence of the conjugal happiness of Antonia and Drusus is immortalized on the bas-relief of the *Ara Pacis,* where Augustus' family appears in a slow procession.

The love of Agrippina and Germanicus is even more celebrated, thanks to Tacitus, who asserts that married love softened Agrippina's indomitable temperament!

But the two princes died tragically and prematurely. Antonia withdrew into austere widowhood, devoting herself to the education of her children and grandchildren; she cultivated friendships and managed her immense fortune but avoided apparent political activity. Agrippina, on the other hand, brandished her widowhood like a weapon against Tiberius, and on the pretext of avenging her husband and safeguarding her children's rights, she became the center of antigovernment agitation.

Marriages that turned out badly were the most common; but this society had refinements. Augustus' daughter and granddaughter were convicted of adultery. Though we do not know much about the latter, the ancient authors took pleasure in recounting the excesses of the former. Would she not go to the Forum at night, near the statue of Marsyas where the prostitutes gathered, to use her right to 'try everything'? As for Messalina, Claudius' wife, her name has become the symbol of

debauchery. On pain of death one resisted her, and the easiness of her adulteries disgusted her. She sought, it was said, for 'unknown pleasures,' of which scandal was certainly the most potent. She surrounded her last adultery with unheard-of publicity, calling on her lover accompanied by the entire court, following him everywhere. One day, she installed a part of the palace furnishings at his house. Finally, to crown this unbridled passion, she married him publicly during one of Claudius' visits to Ostia!

Nero's marriage to his cousin and adoptive sister Octavia, one of the last family marriages, was particularly unsuccessful. This time, the wife was the victim. The marriage had been arranged by Agrippina the Younger, within the framework of the whole series of intrigues she carried on to raise her son to the imperial throne. Octavia, the daughter of Claudius, the reigning emperor, had been engaged to a boy of the Silanus family who was descended from the two Julias. As soon as Agrippina succeeded in getting herself married to Claudius, this engagement was broken off. Silanus had to kill himself, and Octavia was married to Nero as a sign of alliance. Once emperor, Nero never came to an understanding with his young wife. Was this because the marriage had been imposed on him? Octavia's nobility and virtue left him cold. At first, to the relief of the great families who feared for their offspring, and to the fury of his mother, he formed a liaison with a slave, Actë. Poppaea, the wife of a friend, thereafter took possession of his heart. Octavia lived quietly in the background, in spite of the popular and domestic discontent woven around her. But after the murder of Agrippina, her mother-in-law, the young wife lost all possible protection. Poppaea wanted to get married. Nero first rejected Octavia on the pretext of sterility; then an accusation of adultery was leveled against her, which authorized her banishment to Pandataria. Finally a rumor was started that she wanted to marry Plautus, a descendant of Augustus. So she was killed; she was twenty years old and vainly protested her innocence.

If Octavia's story shows that it was not always desirable to be a woman of imperial blood, it also proves that the pursuit of imperial marriages sometimes involved serious political consequences. Poppaea had wished to be married. How many others would try to take political advantage of their marriages? Agrippina the Younger, also, after using her art to get Claudius to marry her, seeing that her husband regretted it and fearing the

FROM THE SEVEN HILLS
TO THE SEVENTH ART:

Caesar and Cleopatra.
Julius Caesar.
Quo Vadis?
Nero's Weekend.

consequences of that frame of mind, went ahead and poisoned him to be on the safe side: a dish of mushrooms, a delicacy he liked, precipitated the Emperor's death.

'. . . Is it not the greatest of blessings,' said Augustus, 'to have a good wife, faithful to her hearth, managing her house, raising her children, giving us joy when we are in good health and caring for us when we are ill?'

> She shares our good fortune and comforts us in adversity, she tempers the violence of a young man and softens the austerity of a weary old one . . . Is it not sweet to carry a child in one's arms, to nourish and educate him? Issue of the married couple, he is the reflection of our body, he is the image of our soul; another self may be seen growing in him. Is it not a blessing in quitting this life, to leave in one's house a successor, an heir to one's fortune and one's race; to find, when life fades, a new life continuing, never to fall, as in war, to a stranger's power, not wholly to perish?

When Augustus addressed these words to the knights, was he expressing regrets, or had he no other purpose than to combat the Roman lack of enthusiasm for founding families?

More than a century before the empire, in 131 B.C., Quintus Metellus the Macedonian already exclaimed, 'Senators! If we could remain without wives, we would spare ourselves all this trouble. But since Nature is organized in such a way that we cannot live peaceably with them, nor live at all without them, it is better to think of perpetuating our race than of gaining a few moments of pleasure.' Unfortunately, this sage advice, often repeated – and in the last instance by Augustus – had not been followed. Indeed, celibacy appeared to be the ideal solution; at the end of his days, the aged celibate, after an unhampered life, was still flattered, courted, honored and nursed by a numerous train who hoped for bequests. It is easy to understand, then, the formidable population crisis which raged in the Roman Empire and finally brought about its fall.

The civil wars and the proscriptions had decimated the great families. Another scourge was added to these: the lowering of the birth rate. It is not possible here to discuss the problem of population in modern terms. Ancient demography is not well known. It was, moreover, not a matter of statistics but of issues which troubled the rulers of the time.

The steady reduction of the population required a constant renewal of the ranks of the army, the civil service, the senate, and even of the government by importation from outside. The imperial families added to their number in provinces progressively further removed from Rome. The fall of the Roman Empire is largely explained by the contrast between barbaric peoples eager for land, relatively numerous and warlike, and the sparse and peaceable population of the Roman world.

But we have not yet reached that point. In the period where we are now, recognition was given the problem, and attempts were made to solve it. It was a question of encouraging the Romans of good family to marry and procreate.

To the lowering of the 'marriage rate' was added voluntary sterility. 'I, provide a soldier for the glory of the country? A soldier shall never be born of my blood!' exclaims one of Propertius' heroes. Roman society soon numbered more men than women. This is what Ovid cries when he deplores Corinna's abortion, in terms that indicate the frequency of the act:

Corinna, rashly seeking to rid her heavy bosom of its load, lies languishing in peril of life. Surely for trying without my knowledge a course so filled with danger she merits my anger; but my anger falls before my fear. And yet, either 'twas I that caused her trouble – or so I believe; with me, what might be oft is held for truth . . . you, too, though you were to be born fair, would have perished had your mother tried what you have tried; and I myself, though a death through love was to be my better fate, would never have seen the day had my mother slain me . . . . Why cheat the full vine of the growing cluster, and pluck with ruthless hand the fruit yet in the green? What is ripe will fall of itself – let grow what has once become quick; a life is no slight reward for a short delay . . . oft she who slays her own in her bosom dies herself. She dies herself, and is borne to the pyre with hair unloosed, and all who behold cry out: ' 'Tis her desert!' . . . Ye gods of mercy, grant she has sinned this once in safety, 'tis all I ask; for a second fault, let her bear her punishment!

Another factor in depopulation was infant mortality: throughout the history of the imperial family we find numerous cases of infant mortality which seem natural. Antonia and Drusus had many children of whom only three survived. Neither the son of Julia and Tiberius, nor Caesar's grandchild lived long. The daughter of Nero and Poppaea, who was worshipped as a goddess from birth, died before she was four months old. Deaths in childbirth and the death of infants were doubtless no more frequent than in the rest of antiquity, but here they take on a special prominence.

To remedy these evils, Caesar and Augustus worked out a very strict set of laws: Unmarried women under forty-five were forbidden to wear jewels or be carried in a litter. Daughters had to be provided with proper dowries, sons might marry without their father's consent. Celibates of marriageable age suffered economic difficulties (inability to receive an inheritance). Widows of two years' standing, women divorced more than a year and a half, and married couples without children were considered celibates. In the case of a legacy, these 'celibates' had an interval of one hundred days in which to marry or adopt a child.

In other respects, besides the subsidies granted to large families, the parents of children were in a position above common rights. In progressing along the *cursus honorum* a man had the benefit of one year per child taken off the age requirement. There was precedence among the consuls according to the number of their children. As for women, maternity elevated their status. Freedwomen were relieved of all guardianship and had the right to honors, while those already free achieved great independence. Finally, adultery was punished very severely: the adulterous woman and her partner were deprived of their possessions and banished.

Until that time, the husband, judge in his own house according to ancient family right, extracted from his wife and her lover whatever vengeance he wished.

It is worth your while, ye who would have disaster wait on adulterers, to hear how on every side they fare ill, and how for them pleasure is marred by much pain, and rare as it is, comes off amid cruel perils. One man has thrown himself headlong from the roof; another has been flogged to death; a third in his flight has fallen into a savage gang of robbers, another has paid a price to save his life; another been abused by stable boys.

Still, according to Horace, a courtesan provided less danger.

With her one wasn't apprehensive, at the supreme moment, of a disagreeable shock:

... A husband may rush back from the country, the door burst open, the dog bark, the house ring through and through with the din and clatter of his knocking; the woman, white as a sheet, will leap away, the maid in league with her cry out in terror, she fearing for her limbs, her guilty mistress for her dowry, and I for myself. With clothes disheveled and bare of foot, I must run off dreading disaster in purse or person or at least repute. To be caught is an unhappy fate ...

Maternity.

This last sentence is revealing: the society of the period had become tolerant of these escapades, but 'you must not get caught.' The law encouraged informers but did not bring about much change.

How did the women of the imperial family obey these laws and did they practice what they preached? Certain of them, whose lives were well known to everyone, served actually as examples in reverse. Livia, who should have been the living application of Augustus' ideas; Livia, whose every action had been presented publicly to the senate as the model to imitate, failed in her duty to augment the population: her union with Augustus was stricken with sterility, and she did not have the three children which by this time constituted a numerous family. However, as a consolation after the death of her second son, Drusus, an exception was made to grant her the privileges reserved for mothers of three. And everybody soon came along to the offices of the chancellery to claim a right which had been vainly solicited from nature!

Augustus' niece Antonia the Younger, the inconsolable widow of Drusus, retired to the country and lived alone until her death, in violation of the law which commanded widows to remarry after two years. It is true that she had had many children, of whom three survived, to whose education she devoted herself. In this she followed the example of Atia, the so-effective mother of Octavius.

This Atia, who died very young, seems to have had a great influence on her son, as much through the education she gave him as through her own personality. Widowed by Octavius' father, she had been remarried to Philippus, a man of consular rank, but meanwhile she knew how to surround the children of her first marriage with a family atmosphere. The education she gave her son has often even been extolled as the standard education of antiquity. She took great care of the child, and every evening she asked the tutors and supervisors in charge of him about the way in which he had spent the day and the state of his progress. This constant surveillance applied to amusements as much as to work. Even when as an adolescent of fifteen he assumed the toga of manhood and became a pontiff, the mother did not relax her discipline:

Although he had been registered as of age according to law, his mother no more wanted him to leave home than when he

had been a child; she caused him to follow the same mode of life and he slept in the same room as before. The law, however, made him a man with the right to be treated differently from children . . . . He went to the temples on the proper occasions, but at night, because his youthful charm and splendid rank attracted many women. Though often tempted by them, he never yielded to their charms. The precautions of his mother, who watched over him and never let him go out for long, and his personal prudence on the other hand, protected him even as he grew older.

The austerity and rigor which Augustus was later to affect, the strict education which he provided for his daughter and granddaughters certainly had their origins with Atia.

A watchful mother, she had sufficient authority to guide her son's first political steps. When Caesar, in 47 B.C., fought in Europe, conquered Pompey in Macedonia, took Egypt, crossed from Syria to the Euxine Sea and prepared to enter Africa to end the war, Octavius would have liked to go with him to learn the

profession of arms, but '. . . his mother Atia opposed it and he stayed home.' This feeling of maternal solicitude even drove Atia to accompany her son to Spain a year later when he finally did leave to join Caesar. But this time he succeeded in getting free of her. When he returned, he lodged away from his mother's house, but he took his meals and spent his time there.

Then came Caesar's murder; Octavius was finishing his studies at Apollonia when a letter came from his mother, giving him the news and advising him to return. 'She said that he now must conduct himself like a man, reflect upon what he would do and make plans for action in accordance with circumstances and his fate.' He was indeed the son of such a mother, who was at once prudent – she momentarily advised him to reject the title of adoptive son and heir of Caesar – and ambitious. When Octavius declared that he must avenge Caesar, he failed to persuade his stepfather, who believed that nothing was worth more than a peaceful life. As for Atia, she rejoiced in such a brilliant chance, in the prospective grandeur and power of her son, but she was aware of the danger of such a position. The tragic end of his

Ancient education.

uncle, Caesar, disheartened her. 'Prey to innumerable cares, she sometimes tortured herself by estimating the dangers hanging over the head of anyone aspiring to sovereign power, at other times she was transported with joy in thinking of the authority and immense honors which awaited her son.' Once convinced, 'she urged him to the accomplishment of his design under the auspices of fortune . . . . But she counseled him to use guile, patience, and dissimulation rather than daring or trust.'

Atia died a year after Caesar, but she left her strong imprint upon her son.

In many cases, however, women other than their mothers brought up the children: stepmothers and grandmothers, like Livia for Julia and her offspring, like Agrippina the Younger for Octavia and Britannicus, like Antonia the Younger for Germanicus' children; or older cousins, like Domitia Lepida who had charge of Nero and toward whom Agrippina the Younger conceived a fierce jealously. She thought his cousin spoiled and coaxed him unduly, and that the two pedagogues she had engaged for him, a barber and a dancer, were not exercising a good influence on the child. Agrippina forgot that Domitia Lepida had taken Nero in when he was penniless, orphaned by his father, and bereft of his mother, who had been banished through the good offices of his uncle, the Emperor Caligula. At the death of Domitius Ahenobarbus, Nero's father, Caligula, joint heir to his estate, had seized the whole of the dead man's fortune and then had exiled his sister Agrippina on the grounds of adultery. This story shows why it was sometimes stepmothers, grandmothers, aunts or cousins who raised the children: the mothers often had trouble with the emperors and were deported, generally on the pretext of adultery.

The law concerning adultery had a diverse fate. In certain cases where politics were involved, adultery was punished with the penalties specified by law. Such was the lot of the two Julias, daughter and granddaughter of Augustus. The elder Julia's love affairs were the laughingstock of the whole city. No one was unaware of them, not even her husband Tiberius. When her father Augustus finally learned of them, his anger was so violent and he felt such irritation about them that instead of hiding his sorrow at home he told the senate about it. Then he deported his daughter to the island of Pandataria, off Campania, and refused to recall her in spite of the supplications of the people. She died there, several months after her father. Julia the Younger underwent a similar fate and died after twenty years of exile on the island of Trimeria, after Augustus in his anger had had her house torn down, confiscated her property, and forbidden recognition of any of her children. The dramatic end of these two women for whom no mercy was possible seems nonetheless an echo of the internal political rivalries of the palace, since Augustus permitted, at the same time, the pardon of a certain number of wives condemned for the same offense.

After Augustus' death, the law concerning adultery served essentially to get rid of women who were considered inconvenient. Caligula forced his sisters into incest, prostituted them to his favorites, and then banished them on the pretext of adultery. Nero's wife Octavia and Caligula's cousin Julia experienced the same fate. It was a good way for the sovereign to enrich himself, since he always confiscated the property to his own advantage. As for Messalina, if her adulteries brought about her fall, it was only because they were the cause of the conspiracy hatched against her by the freedmen of her husband, the Emperor Claudius.

But all this is a side issue to the main point: did these ladies have numerous children? To judge by the results, a sort of competition appears to have existed among the young women of the family in Augustus' time. Octavia had been the mother of five children; the two Antonias, her daughters, each had three who survived. In the following generation, Livilla, who was married to Tiberius' son Drusus, also had three children. We learn that her sister-in-law Agrippina the Elder, Germanicus' wife, surpassed her in both beauty and fecundity: nine children, of whom six survived. This was the record, and the imperial family was conscious of it. The Germanicus-Agrippina marriage was the cherished model in all the discourses on repopulation. When the knights obstinately demanded the abolition of the population laws, Augustus had Germanicus' children led forth in the course of a public spectacle. He presented them, some in his own arms, others in their father's, and made it understood that this was the example to follow. The day of Germanicus' triumph the spectacle was enhanced by the fine bearing of the victorious General and by the sight of his five children riding in his chariot. Agrippina had only to appear with one of her children to provide an image of Ceres, fecundity, the goddess bearing fruit. This surname was often given her. Chastity and fertility: such were the characteristics of Agrippina, extolled as a living example in complete accordance with grandfather Augustus' wishes.

But after the generation that launched the empire, the effort slackened. Agrippina the Younger only became a mother once in all her three marriages. Messalina had only two children, Britannicus and Octavia. At the end of the century, Juvenal says: 'But rarely does a gilded bed contain a woman lying-in: so potent are the arts and drugs of her that can ensure barrenness, and for bribes kill men while yet unborn.' And he adds spite-fully: 'Yet grieve not at this, poor wretch! and with thine own hand give thy wife the potion whatever it be: for did she choose to bear her leaping children in her womb, thou would'st per-chance become the sire of an Ethiop . . . .' The laws were casu-ally evaded by the women of the imperial family, as by all Roman society, which had never really accepted them. Fifty years later the Antonine dynasty could only achieve succession through adoption. Except for Marcus Aurelius, the next to last, none of the emperors had a child.

The Home

While their eventual fruitfulness reserved an important and public role in Roman society for princesses and great ladies, everyday life conferred upon them a considerable domestic power.

Leaving aside the characters exaggerated by satire, let us consider the rich young wife face to face with her responsibilities. On a material level these responsibilities were great. An entire world depended on her: a multitude of slaves, many hangers-on who came to beg favors of her or await her orders, numerous freedmen quick to discharge the missions entrusted to them.

Legions of slaves cultivated her lands, manufactured some of the objects in daily use, and answered every purpose. These were only considered by their number; they were *things* of which she made use as she saw fit. In a pinch they would play the part of submissive and discreet lovers.

You have been made, Cinna, by Marulla the father of seven – not children, for there is no son of yours, nor son of a friend or neighbour; but creatures conceived on truckle-beds and mats betray by their features their mother's adulteries. This one who struts with curly hair, a Moor, confesses he is the offspring of Santra the cook; but that other with flat nostrils, blubber lips is the very image of Pannichus the wrestler. Who is not aware, if he has known and seen the blear-eyed Dama, that the third is the baker's son? The fourth, with his shameless brow, pallid face, was born to you from your minion Lygdus: use your son as you do him, if you wish; 'tis no crime. But

41

this creature with pointed head, and long ears which move just as donkeys' ears are wont – who could deny he is the son of Cyrta the cretin? Two sisters – one is dark, the other red-haired – are the children of Crotus, fluter to the chorus, and of Carpus the bailiff. By now your troupe of slaves would have been made up of as many sons as Niobe's, if Coresus and Dindymus had not been eunuchs.

Slaves gave women a sense of absolute power which could reach the point of suppressing all human feeling in them. Too many known texts insist on unequaled acts of cruelty.

One has rods broken about him, another bleeds from the whips, a third from the cowhide. Some women pay a regular salary to their torturers. While he lashes she is employed in enamelling her face. She listens to her friend's chat, or examines the broad gold of an embroidered robe. Still he lashes. She pores over the items in her long diary. Still he lashes. Until at length, when the torturers are exhausted, 'Begone!' she thunders out in awful voice, the inquisition being now complete.

Most to be pitied among the slaves were the waiting-women, and of those the one who filled the delicate role of hairdresser. 'I hate those women,' wrote Ovid, 'who scratch their hairdresser's face with their fingernails, or take a pin from their hair and plunge it into her arm.' Juvenal describes the martyrdom of poor Psecca, one day when her mistress wished to be beautiful; hair down, shoulders bare, breast uncovered, she is arranging the lady's coiffure: 'Why is this curl too high? Instantly the cowhide avenges the heinous crime of the misplacing of a hair.' Later, Martial recounts: 'One curl of the whole round of hair had gone astray, badly fixed by an insecure pin. This crime Lalage avenged with the mirror in which she had observed it, and Plecusa, smitten, fell because of those cruel locks.'

Yet it is permissible to observe this scene on a less tragic day. The position which slaves sometimes occupied near the great ladies was the more considerable the higher the lady's rank in society. The slaves of Livia and Antonia the Younger played a political role, sometimes to their cost. Acme, one of Livia's Jewish slave-girls, was the agent of a whole conspiracy hatched against Herod, the King of the Jews, by his son Antipater. The

"The delicate role of hairdresser."

latter had bribed Acme to send letters to Herod which she claimed to have found among Livia's correspondence. The plot was discovered, and Acme paid for her willingness with her life; but many other slaves, having succeeded in intrigues of this kind, were freed by their mistress and achieved fine careers! The most complete success must undoubtedly be credited to Cenis. Former secretary to Antonia, who freed her, she became the mistress and then the wife of the Emperor Vespasian. There existed cases of boundless devotion and fidelity of slaves toward their mistress: those of Nero's wife Octavia always refused in spite of tortures to say anything that might compromise her.

In ancient times the number of slaves seems fabulous, judging by the precise duties of many of them: torch- and lantern-bearers, litter bearers and guides, footmen for street escort, wardrobe flunkeys for dressing, a slave to announce the hour, nomenclators who kept names and addresses, secretaries, social secretaries and finally those whose beauty or wit adorned banquets.... But wait! Less than three centuries ago in France, a woman of quality had to manage a household of at least seventy-five persons. A simple magistrate in 1675 kept a secretary, a stableman, two manservants, a doorkeeper, a steward, a major-domo, a kitchenmaid, two pages, six lackeys, two coachmen, two footmen, two carriageboys, four grooms, and for Madame's private use, two maids, a lady's maid, and four servant girls ....

So far we have spoken only of slaves. To the slaves must be added the freedmen and hangers-on. It is not astonishing with all this that the great ladies overburdened their stewards or stewardesses, on whom they were tempted to unload the responsibility of such a vast world. It is not astonishing that they also often had recourse to the good offices of a 'general agent,' who advised them and helped them to manage their fortunes. Attorneys, those indispensable personages who were always in the shadow of the patroness, seemed to men to be 'absurd and insipid creatures in the society of men, but astute and perfect legal experts among women.' They sometimes became confidants whose influence could be profound, judging by certain inscriptions: 'I was Lepida's attorney, and I controlled her affairs. While I lived she remained Caesar's daughter-in-law.' This Lepida had been engaged to one of Augustus' grandsons. As it turned out she married several times; her last husband was a rich old man without children. She was accused in 20 A.D. of having simulated the birth of a child of this marriage. Like all matters involving women at that time, this one was grafted onto a charge of adultery, poisoning, and sorcery. If one believes Tacitus, who draws the portrait of this cruel delinquent, the attorney must have had a good deal on his hands! In any case, this personage was always there. His activities often seem precarious when, as an interested party, the young and handsome man at the same time played the role of the lady's lover. He soon became a character in literature. The handsome attorney, the attorney with curled hair, toward whom the husband is obliged to behave with all consideration. Martial gives a charming picture of him:

> Who is that curled spark who is always clinging to your wife's side, Marianus? Who is that curled spark, who whispers some trifle into the lady's tender ear, and leans on her chair with his right elbow, round each of whose fingers runs a light ring, who carries legs unmarred by any hair? ... 'That individual does my wife's jobs,' you say. To be sure! ... He does your wife's jobs, does he? ... That fellow doesn't do your wife's jobs: he does yours.

The lady was in command of this entire staff of subordinates. Or rather, she reigned. The respectful terms used to address her attest to this. Her husband sometimes might call her *Domina* – 'mistress,' an expression lacking the banality of 'madam.' In great families the father was called *Dominus*, and Augustus accomplished a kind of minor revolution by forbidding his grandsons to give him this title, even as a joke. 'Master' and 'mistress' really kept their original respectful meanings. To the name *Domina*, another sometimes was added: *Regina*. It was used by the hangers-on.

At the beginning of the empire, life at home was supposed to be guided by the slogan of the first imperial court: frugality, parsimony, austerity. These three words, which constantly reappear under the admiring pens of ancient authors, are not well suited to the actual growth of Roman luxuriousness, which did not cease to develop throughout a century and a half and reached its apogee at the end of the Julio-Claudian dynasty with the Golden House of Nero, in which one room was completely lined with fine pearls.

The emperor, of course, set the example of austerity; he soon set the example for having beautiful buildings constructed. Ori-

ginally, the prince's dwelling was hardly distinguishable from that of a rich private citizen. Augustus at first lodged in the house of the orator Hortensius, Cicero's rival; it was given the name of palace because it was situated on the Palatine Hill, and in Rome there was a whole tradition about the Palatine. Romulus and the kings of Rome were supposed to have lived there. Thus the early days of the republic attached an evil reputation to that part of the city. For the great figures of the republic, wanting to live there meant being suspected of aspiring to royalty. Then, following the example of democratic leaders whom one could not reasonably suspect, people began to build there. From a parvenu neighborhood, it became Rome's fashionable quarter before it was the imperial seat.

From Hortensius' house there was a splendid view overlooking the city: the Capitol, the Aventine with its gardens and temples, the Campagna and the magnificent monuments of the Via Appia, and finally the hills at the edge of the Tiber. The house itself, very modest at first, contained neither marble nor mosaics. The only embellishments were moderate porticoes supported by stone columns. As his wealth increased, Augustus bought a certain number of houses surrounding his own. He had them demolished and dedicated part of the land to the construction of religious buildings: the Temple of Apollo and notably two magnificent libraries, Greek and Latin. But at the same time the prince's house was transformed and enlarged. After its destruction in a fire caused by lightning, a palace replaced it. Temples surrounded it, a circle of oak trees shaded the gate, and laurels were planted on both sides of the door.

This was the period when the best building was done. From that time on marble was used, which was brought from the Alban Hills and Carrara and then from Numidia. The plan of the traditional Greco-Roman house was faithfully retained: one story overlooked an interior court lined with columns onto which the rooms opened. But the edifices were enlarged and multiplied. The dwelling covered a space all the more extensive for including a garden, a park, and numerous secondary accessories: baths, colonnades, picture galleries, paths for chariots. On the other hand, the living rooms stayed rather small. Their shape varied according to the architect's inspiration; there were square and rectangular ones, but also round and octagonal. We know this to be true particularly of Augustus' house.

Ostentatious display appeared in architectural decoration:

47

Livia's house.

colored marbles for columns, walls paneled with enormous plaques of precious marbles which vied with each other in brilliance, mosaics mounted with rare and fine stones – alabaster, porphyry, granite, green ophite. Variety of color was the essential element in this ornamentation. The floors were paved with mosaic, and the ceilings were painted. For total effect, these houses sought coolness. They wished to give an impression of greenery, due as much to their decoration as to the gardens surrounding them.

The pleasure garden included the various elements of French formal gardens, which were to reconstruct it on a grandiose scale. It was conceived as an architectural composition leading from the house to the countryside, the latter often being represented by a *trompe l'oeil* painting on a distant wall. The gardens contained an arrangement of sculptures and edifices – grottoes, colonnades, and pavilions were carefully distributed among elements of greenery which were situated according to three different vertical forms: columns or tall trees (plane trees, cypresses) connected by garlands of creeping plants lined the paths or the flower beds; bushes (usually box) were forced by strict pruning into geometric shapes, the forms of wild animals or the shape of the owner's signature; finally, beds of flowers were spread out in profuse variety but limited to a small number of species, principally roses, lilies, and violets. The essential purpose was to make especial use of water in all its forms: river, lake, pool, fountain, or simple spring.

The furniture in these dwellings would scarcely answer to our needs: we live sitting down, the Romans lived reclining. Beds – single, double, triple or sextuple – were the essential articles of furniture. They answered all purposes – eating, sleeping, receiving visitors, writing. Triple or sextuple beds were used at large dinners, double ones were for married couples, single ones for every purpose. Stools, mostly unused, were no more than easily transportable 'camp chairs'; the armchair was the privilege of the gods, and soon also that of emperors and their wives at certain official receptions. The chair, very unusual, was used by some ladies. As for tables, their function approached that of elegant pedestals on which to display ornaments, the signs of wealth. Ebony chests protected the clothing. Luxury appeared in embellishment and in the materials used: ivory, silver, rich fabrics, rare carpets.

In this setting where, as we have seen, an abundant staff of

servants moved about, what were the woman's occupations? Quite often she might want to relegate household cares to her steward and devote herself only to tempting pursuits; idleness would indeed have much charm for her. But it would be a mistake to think that the great lady remained inactive in her own home. She had exact duties.

The true Roman matron of the period was Livia, who ruled the *Domus Palatina* where a vast part of the emperor's family and 'friends' lived, among these the children of allied kings who had been invited to come and be educated in Rome along with the children of the house. Undoubtedly, Livia was not content to entrust the task of administering the entire household to a steward. She saw and knew everything. Every day she herself apportioned the tasks, and according to the ancient custom set the amount of wool to be spun. The spinning and weaving of the wool and the making of clothes for men and women were counted among the most important household activities. The mistress of the house was expected to take part in them. Livia attempted to strengthen and invigorate this tradition, which was tending to die out in high society: Augustus wore only garments made by his wife, sister, daughter, or granddaughters.

There are many documents which attest to the importance of women's manual work. Spinning and weaving are the great concern of the ladies of the period, says Musonius Rufus, a Stoic philosopher of the first century. Funerary epitaphs, intended to signify the virtues and perfections of a dead lady, sometimes bear the representation of a loom. A former consul, singing the praises of his deceased wife Turia, inscribed on her tomb, amid other virtues common to all women, her tireless skill in the art of spinning and weaving wool. Even women of the demimonde – Propertius' Cynthia, Tibullus' Delia – were far from avoiding the custom. Tibullus evokes the happy moment when he sees his beloved again after a long separation. Delia is sitting by her lamp, spinning, despite the lateness of the hour; an old woman's tales keep her awake; the eyes of the servant girls spinning with her are almost closing, when she suddenly jumps up at her lover's appearance and runs to meet him, with bare feet and disheveled hair . . . .

Among the other activities that traditionally devolved upon women, there remains the education of children, at least in part. Children were taken along everywhere . . . even unborn ones. The number of members of the imperial family born outside of

Rome or Italy is considerable. To cite only a few examples, Antonia was born in Greece, Claudius at Lyons, Agrippina the Elder and her daughter Julia at Mitylene on the island of Lesbos, and Agrippina the Younger in Germania.

The local population always welcomed the presence of these children in any part of the Roman Empire: they were included in the honors conferred upon their parents.

What were little girls taught? How did they spend the twelve or fifteen years of childhood while they lived in their mother's house?

First came infancy, dolls, colored balloons. Then the age of stories: these were like ours. 'Once upon a time there was a king and queen . . .' the same wonderful formula. The heroine was always endowed with incomparable beauty. A princess, she was usually the youngest, exposed to the jealousy of older sisters less beautiful than she, who constantly tormented her. Fortunately, helpful supernatural beings came to put an end to the innumerable troubles she suffered. If a heroine, victim of her harsh mistress' insults, had to finish sorting out a huge heap of grain by the end of the day, the ants came to finish the work in her stead; the eagle came to draw miraculous water for her from the spring guarded by dragons. Of course, the stories always came out all right, the obstacles were overcome, the beauty married the charming prince, and the wicked were punished with violent death.

The difference between our children's stories and those which charmed the ears of young Romans lies in the personal intervention of the gods. The Romans, following the Greeks, attributed feelings to them as varied and sometimes as base as those of human beings. This is notably true in the lovely tale of Cupid and Psyche, where Venus replaces the wicked fairy.

But soon more serious instruction had to be thought of. In the class of society we are dealing with, the little girl, like the little boy, received her education at home and not at the public school. Sometimes mothers undertook it themselves, but usually they were satisfied to choose preceptors to direct the education of the children. It seems there was scarcely any concern about the dangers which might result from this instruction. Nevertheless, Seneca, the 'preceptor' of Germanicus' youngest daughter, was to be banished by Caligula for a rather dishonorable reason. A similar suspicion hung over the celebrated pedagogue Q. Caecilius Epirota, freedman of Atticus and tutor of Pom-

Cupid and Psyche.

ponia, Agrippa's first wife. Roman girls, like Greek women, were married so young that their education was often completed in their husband's home.

Feminine instruction rested on three fundamentals: study of the classics, needlework, and the art of pleasing. The cultivation of the intellect was quite thorough. First, of course, one learned to read and write; these two subjects were undertaken together with sensible slowness: the alphabet, backward and forward, the pairing of letters, syllables, isolated words. Little texts were learned by heart and recited, and some very simplified notions of arithmetic were given. It is still more interesting that Greek was taught at the same time as Latin. This culture was bilingual like that of France in the seventeeth century, when Latin and French were taught concurrently. And so our Roman ladies read Greek. They knew Homer and the comic poet Menander; the constant allusions to Greek mythology which are scattered through the works of Latin poets – and are the despair of schoolboys – were easily understood by Roman girls. 'Let the Muse of Callimachus and the Coan bard be known to you, and the old drunkard's Teian strains; let Sappho too be known (for who more wanton than she?), or he whose sire is deceived by the crafty Getan's cunning . . .' recommends Ovid to his pupils in *The Art of Love.*

The study of Greek and Latin texts was the foundation of secondary schooling. There were basic authors. The unexcelled orator was Cicero, to the exclusion of all others. He was to be cultivated and imitated. The dramatic author was Terence, the historian, Sallust. Neither Caesar's limpid style nor the monumental official work of Titus Livy found favor with teachers at that time. But the study of the poets remained the essential part of every education. For a long time the Romans had at their disposal only old Ennius; in 26 B.C., under the influence of Q. Caecilius Epirota, fashionable poets were introduced into the program. They began with Vergil: 'And you should be able to read . . . of Aeneas the wanderer, origin of lofty Rome, a work than which none more famous has appeared in Latium . . .'

Vergil thus became the Homer of the Latins. The poets might be discussed throughout an entire dinner. Juvenal complains: 'Nothing is more tedious than women, who, barely at table, start to praise Vergil, justify Dido's death, place the poets on a parallel and compare Vergil to Homer.' To Vergil was added Horace, another actually official poet. He wrote a hymn to order for the Emperor Augustus which was sung at the Secular Games by twenty-seven girls and twenty-seven boys of the nobility. To these poets, following the advice of their profuse Ovid in *The Art of Love,* the older girls undoubtedly added the tender lines of Propertius, those of the beloved Tibullus, some passages of Gallus, and the poem composed by Varro on that golden fleece

53

so fatal to Phrixus' sister. Ovid ends by saying of himself:

> Perhaps too my name will be joined to theirs, nor will my writings be given to Lethe's waters; and someone will say, 'Read the elegant poems of our master, wherein he instructs the rival parties; or from the three books marked by the title of *Loves* choose out what you may softly read with docile voice.'

But as for Ovid and *The Art of Love,* that was a study of a different kind – a study which, if one is to believe Horace, virgins undertook too soon. The arts of pleasing had their place there. In spite of the Roman's small taste for music and dancing, it was proper for a young girl to know how to sing. The woman who wished to please had to know how 'to hold her quill in her right hand and her lyre in her left hand.' She also had to know how to dance. At the time, dancing consisted chiefly of a rhythmic swinging of the upper body and the arms. However, although the practice of these skills was indispensable, there was a strict limit: the loose dances of Ionia and the psaltery, an instrument favorable to love, were not suitable for virgins.

This predominantly literary and artistic education sometimes gave a profound cultivation to those women who profited by it. The imperial family once more provides us with numerous examples of that agreeable and feminine pastime, literature.

It was good form to speak a Latin larded with Greek words, better to pass oneself off as an authentic Athenian. Juvenal exclaims furiously:

> Everything is in Greek! How disgraceful it is for our countrywomen not to know their mother tongue! In this language they give vent to their fears, their anger, their joys and cares, and all the inmost workings of their souls . . . . This in young girls you may excuse. But must thou, forsooth, speak Greek, that hast had the wear and tear of six and eighty years? In an old woman this language becomes immodest . . .

But there are lofty examples: the correspondence of Augustus and Livia is studded with Greek words and citations borrowed from Hellenic literature.

Julia was well educated, and she also cultivated a love of literature. Her witticisms were celebrated in Rome. For a long

54

time her wit allowed her to reply triumphantly to paternal admonitions. Agrippina the Elder, her daughter, received advice from Grandfather Augustus about style: 'Be careful,' he instructs her, 'not to write and speak with affectation.' The second Julia, Agrippina's sister, was a great friend of the poet Ovid. This friendship was fatal to the writer, for he was exiled at the same time as she. The poet of *The Art of Love*, who depicts for us the women of the time with such grace and such cynicism, was regarded as a public poisoner by the Emperor. All the ladies of the aristocracy knew his work by heart, and perhaps it was only they who read it. Ovid was considered a 'woman's writer': nevertheless, he was the author of the moment. Finally, 'the family' included at least one woman writer in the person of Agrippina the Younger, who wrote her memoirs.

Even outside of the imperial family, we have many proofs of the taste shown by women for letters, which was not, however, entirely separate from song. It seems common for women to have been capable of setting poems to music. Of course, they also wrote them, as in the present day. Ovid's daughter, Perilla, was a poetess. Of course masculine colleagues ridiculed 'learned women.' Listen to Juvenal:

> May the woman who shares your bed never have her own personal style, never fire off a tortuous syllogism in rounded phrases, may she fail to know something in history, and fail to understand everything she reads .... I abhor a woman who ceaselessly reels off and repeats the method of Palaemon without ever disobeying the rules of the language, who, obsessed with erudition, quotes me lines I do not know, and, for an ignorant woman friend, points out mistakes that men would not notice. I wish a husband had the right to commit a solecism.

In a more serious vein, the ladies were also interested in philosophy. One, like Octavia, might have a treatise dedicated to her, another possess 'her' philosopher or philosophers: they played something like the part of a father confessor. These individuals, often bearded, sometimes devoted themselves to astrology or 'mathematics'; Poppaea was always accompanied by 'mathematicians' ready to predict the future for her. Livia, after the death of Drusus, was consoled – entirely honorably – by the philosopher Areus, a friend of her husband's.

"These ladies were also interested in philosophy."

Novels were also read. The fashionable authors included a Milesian, Aristippus. The titles of certain works of his have come down to us: *The Mirror of Lais; The Loves of Anthias and Habracome;* finally, *Milesian Fables,* a collection of Oriental tales on various racy subjects. These stories were set in Miletus, a city in Asia Minor which had the privilege of supplying the harems of Oriental sovereigns – they must have been like *The Thousand and One Nights.*

To have a fine library was highly desirable. Books were stacked in great cedar chests called *armoria*. The books appeared in the form of thin installments bound in covers dyed with rose madder, with the title in vermilion. The cedar oil protected the leaves from the attacks of worms and moths – but not from the grocers, who later used them to wrap olives or tuna fish! These books were also very expensive, despite the use of slave labor – which explains the use of dummy bindings in libraries. In the last century a magnificent chased silver casket was unearthed at Pompeii. By its appearance (a polygon surmounted by the nine Muses), it was a standard example of a traveling library, hermetically sealed with a lock. Imagine the emotion of the archaeologist counting on a treasure of Latin literature . . . . When he finally got around to opening the casket, he found a collection of little pots full of rouge!

The elegant lady who thus baffled our archaeologist leads us to one of the most important preoccupations of the lady at home: dress. At the beginning of a treatise devoted to 'Cosmetics,' a list of recipes for beauty of which only a fragment remains, Ovid tells us of the part played by dress at that time:

> The Sabine dames of old under king Tatius would perchance have wished to cultivate their paternal acres rather than themselves: when the matron, sitting rubicund in her high seat, spun assiduously with hardened thumb, and herself penned up the lambs her daughter had pastured, herself set the twigs and cleft logs upon the hearth. But your mothers have borne delicate girls. You wish your bodies to be covered with gold-embroidered gowns, you wish to have hands that shine with gems: you adorn your necks with stones sought from the East, and so large that the ear finds two a burden to bear. Nor is that a fault, if you are anxious to please, for men love elegance in these times of ours. In feminine wise are your husbands made trim, and the bride has scarce aught to add to their smartness.

Of course, we must begin with beauty care, the indispensable prelude. Women, if not cosmetics, scarcely change throughout the ages! Husbands took a dim view of the lady's evening mask; 'ridiculous and hideous to see,' the wife's face was swollen with a thick layer of milk and bread crumbs called *poppaeana*. It was in fact the Empress who invented it, among other creations in the field of beauty preparations, to replace a poultice of fat beans.

The fool of a husband would get his lips stuck to this glue. One can easily see that she had to wash her face with a lot of water when she got up in the morning, and what is more, get rid of the rancid odor which these mixtures left behind. To preserve an unfailing freshness and suppleness of the skin, one of the formulas recommended by Ovid was also used: a cream made of wool grease with an asses' milk base, which gave off nauseating odors. It was better to close the door when she devoted herself to these operations!

The hands and ears were washed, and also the teeth, 'lest tartar should attack them.' One gargled with lightly perfumed water, which served to keep the breath fresh and pure. Then came the bath in fragrant water, and the rubdown. The face and body were ready to receive the foundation of vivid color which would cause the last of the night's blemishes to disappear. Ovid, professor of seduction, writes:

Learn now in what manner, when sleep has let go your tender limbs, your faces can shine bright and fair. Strip from its covering of chaff the barley which Libyan husbandmen have sent in ships. Let an equal measure of vetch be moistened in ten eggs, but let the skinned barley weigh two pounds. When this has dried in the blowing breezes, bid the slow she-ass break it on the rough millstone: grind therewith too the first horns that fall from a nimble stag (let the sixth part of a solid pound be added). And now when it is mixed with the dusty grain, sift it all straightway in hollow sieves. Add twelve narcissus-bulbs without their skins, and let a strenuous hand pound them on pure marble. Let gum and Tuscan seed weigh a sixth part of a pound, and let nine times as much honey go to that. Whoever shall treat her face with such a prescription will shine smoother than her own mirror. Nor hesitate to roast pale lupin-seeds, and therewith fry beans that puff out the body; with fair discernment let each have six pounds' weight, give each to the black millstones to be pounded small. Nor let white lead nor foam of red nitre be lacking, nor the iris that comes from Illyrion soil. Give them all alike to be subdued by the strong arms of youths, but when ground their right weight will be one ounce. Spots on the face are banished by a remedy taken from the querulous nest of birds: halcyon-cream they call it. If you ask with what weight thereof I am content, it is that which an ounce divided into two parts weighs. That they may mix and be properly smeared upon the body, add Attic honey from its yellow combs. Although incense appeases the gods and angered powers, it must not all be offered upon kindled altars. When you have mixed incense with nitre that scrapes off warts, see that on either side the balance there is a third of a pound exact. Add a pound, less its fourth part, of gum stripped of its bark, and a moderate cube of juicy myrrh. When you have pounded these up, sift them in close-set meshes: the powder must be settled by pouring honey on it. It has been found useful to add fennel to the fragrant myrrh (let the fennel weigh five scruples, the myrrh nine), and of dry rose-leaves as much as the hand can grasp, and frankincense with salt of Ammon. Thereon pour the juice that barley makes; let rose-leaves and salt together equal the incense in weight. Though it be smeared but for a short time on your soft countenance, a fine colour will remain on all your face . . . .

After the make-up came depilation and the arrangement of the hair. Women were all the more careful of their hair, since the loss of it was ignominious: 'Shameful the shorn herd, the fields without vegetation, the leafless forest, shameful the hairless head.' And so various greases were used. The hair was dyed black like the Britons, or blond like the Germans. The enthusiasm for tinting was so great as to extend to red. Fantastic colors were even adopted, with the exception of the yellow and blue reserved for courtesans. But this fashion was not without disadvantages:

I used to say to you: stop dyeing your hair! And now you have no more hair to dye. Besides . . . there was nothing more beautiful than your hair . . . but its color was certainly not that of ebony, nor that of gold: it was a mixture of both . . . . Although her hair was soft as down, how often, alas! was it subjected to torture! How often did it patiently endure the iron and the fire in order to be twisted into rounded curls! . . . That beautiful hair is no longer comparable to Diana's as she emerged naked from the foam on the waves . . . . Why, if it never pleased you, do you deplore the loss of your hair? Why

"And of dry rose-leaves, as much as the hand can grasp."

do you push away your mirror in a rage? Its fall was not at all the result of a serious illness, nor of a rival's jealousy: no, the fault is your own, you spread the poison on your head yourself. Now Germania will send you the hair of slaves: a conquered nation will shoulder the burden of your headdress. How many times, when you hear praise for the beauty of your hair, will you shamefacedly say to yourself: now it is a

61

purchased adornment which makes me appear beautiful; it is
some Sicambrian who is being admired, not I. And meanwhile
I remember a time when this homage was addressed only to
me.

The use of wigs and false hair seems to have been very common: 'The woman shows herself to you, wearing the thick head
of hair she has just bought, and for a little money other people's
hair becomes her own. She does not even blush to purchase it
publicly, in sight of Hercules and the nine sisters.'

As for hair arrangement itself, it was a great affair. Every
woman 'of the world' was bound to keep following the latest
fashion. If one is to believe Ovid, the great specialist on the
subject, '. . . you will not count the acorns on the oak's numerous
boughs, nor how many bees there are in Hybla, nor wild beasts
upon the Alps; nor can I enumerate all the fashions that there
are: each day adds more adornments.' Meanwhile, a lady had
to choose the coiffure which became her best: 'An oval face
prefers a parting upon the head left unadorned. Round faces

would fain have a small knot left on top of the head, so that the ears show. Let another's locks hang down on either shoulder . . . Let another braid her hair like girt-up Diana . . .' Nevertheless, there were dominant contours, according to the evidence of busts and medallions. In order to follow the changes in fashion, sculptors from whom busts were ordered used a special marble for the hair – and the mode was followed by changing the stone wig! In the first century of our era, the evolution is quite clear, from the sober coiffure which gives refinement to Octavia's face, to the simple ringlets of Agrippina the Elder, and finally to the complicated edifice of Messalina. This was the beginning of the superimposed layers of curls which were to be the delight of the following epoch.

The hair was fastened with shell combs or large pins which might be of gold. It was with one of these golden pins from her hair that Fulvia, when she was unchained, pierced the tongue of Cicero's corpse in vengeance. Sometimes certain of these pins were hollow and could hold poison.

We will refrain from going back to the long and tiring hair-

dressing session, which could prove fatal to the *ornatrix*, and we will take up the subject of make-up. This was contained in little pots and flagons, placed in an easily transportable special casket, which allowed one to make and remake oneself into a beauty. The poet writes spitefully: 'You reside, O Galla, in a hundred pyxes, and the face you show is not the one that sleeps with you.' The colors with which the face was adorned varied according to the state of mind: every woman in love had to be pale; 'it is the only color which is suitable when the heart is enamored: seeing her, everyone should be tempted to exclaim; she is in love.' White lead or chalk came opportunely to the aid of natural pallor, except that one shuns the sun and the other the rain. All women did not wish to give their complexions this 'whiteness of the finest marble,' and they made much use of rouge. It was art that furnished the pale vermilion that the blood denied, Ovid tells us. The Roman ladies used three kinds of rouge: red lead, carmine, and a certain substance extracted from the crocodile. But care had to be taken not to turn this over-painted face into a plaster or an ulcer, not to cause the gorge to rise in disgust at the sight of the scum trickling on the cheeks, drawing them down to the chest with its weight.

The eyes also were the object of careful attention: antimony or black lead shaded the eyelids, lashes and brows. 'Your skill can fill in the spaces in an eyebrow not strongly marked. Do not be afraid to enliven the sparkle of your eyes with fine cinder or with saffron,' Ovid advises continually. Evidently false eyebrows at least were not worn.

Our great lady is washed, made up, and curled; now she is ready to dress!

The terminology of undergarments poses many problems; they seemed to consist of one or two tunics of varying lengths, one on top of the other. In certain cases, the ladies would try to make the waistline thinner, compress the bust, and above all to disguise malformations with the help of pads: but 'A woman must take care to conceal all these things.' And so let us first admire the sober *stola*, which was suitable for all women of matronly status. The *stola* was a long white dress drawn in at the waist and falling to the feet. According to the fashion of the moment, the belt either remained visible or was hidden under a fold. A band of gauze ornamented with jewels or embroidery trimmed the bottom of the dress. This long pleated sheath hid or exposed the arms according to circumstances. At

65

the shoulder the *fibulae*, richly decorated clasps, secured the whole. To go out, the *palla* was thrown over it – a rectangular piece of cloth held at the shoulder by another *fibula*. Horace tells us:

> In a matron one can see only her face, for unless she be a Catia, her long robe conceals all else. But if you seek forbidden charms that are invested with a rampart – for this it is that drives you crazy – many obstacles will then be in your way: attendants, the sedan, hairdressers, parasites, the robe dropping to the ankles, and, covered with a wrap, a thousand things which hinder you from a clear view.

However, this austere but becoming garment, which Livia always wore, and which a woman of questionable morals was not permitted to put on, was not the only one.

There existed all kinds of tunics, of different colors and materials. Wool, silk, and cotton, according to their treatment, produced fabrics more or less light and thin. Lightness and thinness constituted the epitome of elegance. Sea-green, azure-blue, saffron-yellow, and flesh color tinted them with vivid hues; but nothing surpassed Tyrian purple, the color reserved for great occasions. There even existed tunics decorated with floral patterns, strewn with flowers of gold and purple embroidery.

As for footgear, the most common was a shoe of white leather, of which the soles might be thickened for appearing taller.

The most interesting subject in dress is undoubtedly jewelry, and Roman men and women doted on it. Since the victory of Pompey over Mithridates, pearls and precious stones had become the pre-eminent luxury. Among stones the diamond was valued but little used, since the art of cutting it was not understood. Berenice's diamond, mentioned by Juvenal, seemed to be an exception. The most sought-after precious stone was the emerald, of which pendants were made; the acquamarine and opal were also much appreciated. But pearls far outranked the rarest stones. Pearls were worn as earrings; they were embroidered on clothing; they even embellished shoes.

Women thus arrayed themselves in necklaces, pendants, and earrings made of the largest pearls. The most elegant were 'rattlers,' double pendants ending with a pearl, mounted in such a way as to make a pleasant clicking when the beauty passed by. For bracelets, heavy gold fashioned into the form of a

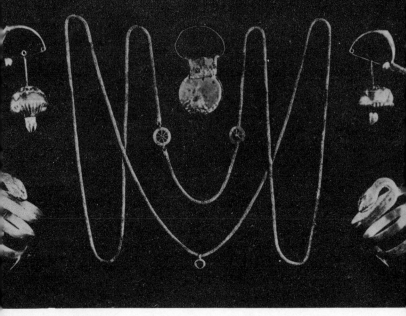

Pompeian jewelry

serpent was the favorite. And finally rings: they were worn in quantity, often several on each finger, over the different joints. Only the middle finger had to remain entirely free, for superstitious reasons. Certain of these rings were intended for the big toe – their weight seems enormous. There was even the coquetry of keeping lighter rings for summer and heavier ones for winter.

The value of these jewels was all the greater if they possessed a history. It was customary to recount the identities of their former owners, mostly conquered kings and queens. Juvenal shows us the capricious and flirtatious woman who ruins her husband: 'After so many remarkable gifts, she was thought to be satisfied. But no, she fumed with impatience to own Berenice's famous diamond, which she thought the more precious because a queen had worn it . . .' It could be said of Lollia Paulina, one of Caligula's wives, that she wore the revenues of an entire province: she was encountered at a betrothal feast in a modest family, flaunting a set of emeralds and pearls which bedizened her whole head, hair, ears, throat, and fingers. The beauty was ready to testify that her set of jewels, 'cash in hand,' was worth forty million sesterces: it was the legacy of her grandfather, who had been a governor in the East.

This kind of display was accompanied by unheard-of extravagances: Antonia the Younger, that sober widow of Drusus, had even conceived the idea of amusing herself by decorating the fish in her ponds with earrings, the better to watch them as they swam in these trappings.

In Society

Roman women always took part in social life; it was a characteristic trait. The matron never remained confined to the house.

The Greek woman of the classical period, in her gynecium, had one ideal: not to be talked about, favorably or otherwise; she did not even go to market: it was the husband who assumed that responsibility, as he did that of all social relationships. If the husband entertained friends, it was in the part of the house reserved for men, the adron, and he received without the presence of his wife, as is still done today in Moslem countries. The Romans never had such an idea. Although it was good form for a Roman woman to remain at home, because domestic occupations sufficed to keep her busy, she was always admitted to banquets and spectacles; and she received in company with her husband.

In fact she went out a great deal, and her social relationships were extremely varied. In the first century, generally speaking, the unwholesome effect of outside activities on her morals was regrettable. But the woman was not solely responsible – men were also depraved. And since they did not conceive of love in the same terms as the Greeks, they involved the women in their pleasures. So of course social relationships that were normally allowed facilitated more illicit intercourse – and a certain moral laxity dwelt on by moralists and satirists. What opportunities to find and to please lovers! What opportunities to choose and seduce mistresses! Reading Ovid's works, *The Art of Love* or *Loves*, books, the author assures us, addressed only to freedmen and courtesans – although we need not believe him – it would be tempting to speak of 'the dunghill of Ennius.' There is a striking resemblance to a certain aspect of the French 'Belle Époque': adultery appears to have been the overwhelming pre-occupation, and love was considered to exist only outside of marriage. But it is too easy to be a malicious gossip: as the satirists took pleasure in being – but such is not our purpose here. The social obligations of the Romans seem fearful to a twentieth-century man. The inferior had to call on his superior, the client on the patron, the beneficiary on his benefactor. He went every day to pay his respects. This consisted of a morning *salutatio,* which was accomplished during the first two hours of the day beginning at dawn, and in full dress. This was an extremely self-seeking visit: one came to solicit a *sportula* (a small basket containing a more or less copious meal), an invitation to dinner, a position, an appointment, a service. The greater the personage receiving in his *atrium,* the greater his influence. In the morning the houses of good Roman society were centers of turmoil, thronged with the most diversified mixture of people. Under the empire, great personages themselves went to perform their *salutatio* – to the emperor, or even to certain members of the imperial family, if they were in Rome. As was the case later at the court of Louis XIV, it was proper 'to be seen.' This custom was a severe drudgery – for the one who came as well as for the one who received – but there was no way to avoid it. The visitor, in order to succeed in gaining admittance, very often had to stand in line, bribe the porter, or suborn the guards. At the imperial court, one was searched, and every pointed object was automatically confiscated. Finally, among equals it was customary to embrace, and the emperor bestowed the traditional kiss upon the senators.

But the women, one would think, had nothing to do with this. These were men's affairs. It does seem that preparing an elaborate toilette occupied the matron in her early morning hours, and not paying or receiving visits. This rule, however, had extremely numerous exceptions. Women did not habitually go along to morning audiences, but there were those who did, and a certain number of them received.

Ladies received the whole multitude who were responsible to them for the management and care of the house; and also, if they were rich widows, many suitors: their age or ugliness notwithstanding, men jostled one another at their gates. Empresses would receive visits from great ladies of the city. Livia and

Agrippina the Younger even received the senate, in an organized body. Otherwise, women occasionally went to the *salutatio*. It was necessary to plead forcefully with Claudius so that women and children who came to the imperial court would not be subjected to the unwholesome contacts of the search. Finally, a widow or a woman attempting to defend her own interests might also occasionally go to the *salutatio,* and not only to the imperial court.

Our great ladies would in general prefer more agreeable ways of passing the time than these more or less official tasks; and perhaps the most popular one was taking the air.

A lady of quality did not go out on foot or alone. She went in a litter or a sedan chair. The litter was a kind of elegant portable sofa, equipped with little posts to which curtains were attached which could be opened an closed at will. The use of this covered litter was in principle reserved for the wives of senators, but in practice, it seems that many infractions of this law were committed. The beauty would lie stretched out on a bed of feathers, her head supported by a soft bolster. It was good form to close the curtains completely, but the husband who insisted on this was considered a brute by his wife, and she passed for a victim of conjugal cruelty! So the curtains most always remained open, and according to Catullus, 'many ladies wore a black veil over their gracious faces . . .' unless they preferred the half-veil, 'so that the portion of the face which was thus hidden urged one to uncover the rest,' insinuates Tacitus. These litters, indeed, were the center of attention for loiterers, who were always ready to hoot at the occupant if her deportment left something to be desired. In Roman traffic passage of this vehicle was difficult; it was preceded by two African runners in white tunics girdled at the waist and with polished silver plaques around their necks; it was carried by eight Syrians dressed as Hercules; and finally some Liburnians in the rear were responsible for keeping the crowd at a distance. The destination of the outing was often a garden where people strolled up and down watching each other go by. Perhaps our elegant lady might then abandon her litter and walk a little, protected by a parasol held by her guard – a eunuch – who occasionally might be replaced by a gallant admirer seizing this chance to begin an intimacy. The prudent young man had only to follow Ovid's advice:

Meanwhile, if she be borne reclining on her cushions, approach your mistress' litter in dissembling fashion, and lest someone intrude hateful ears to your words, hide them so far as you may, in cunning ambiguities; or if the spacious colonnade be trodden by her leisurely feet, do you also make friendly dalliance there . . . Do you yourself hold her parasol outstretched upon its rods, yourself make room for her in the crowd, where she moves . . .

Many outings were dedicated to temple visits. The reasons were diverse, according to what contemporaries spitefully give us to understand. Many ladies affected great piety, but all kinds of adventure could occur in temples . . . .

To follow the Romans in the multiple practices of their various

religious cults is certainly no easy task. In the time of Augustus, Roman polytheism had already been enriched by a series of Oriental cults which appeared little by little in Rome after the Asiatic conquests. The most recent was the Egyptian cult of Isis. By the side of Cybele, the Great Mother who had come from Asia in the second century B.C., Claudius accepted the presence of her lover, Attis. This evolution was continuing at the same time that Judaism spread and Christianity appeared. Let us try to put ourselves into the frame of mind of that time, and banish from our spirits twenty centuries of a monotheistic conception of religion: one universe, one God. The ancient peoples, the Romans especially, were aware of the diversity of the universe; the multiplicity of gods corresponded to the different aspects of nature. Hence the existence of 'specialist' gods: the goddess of childbirth, Lucina, the god of the child's first steps, the god of the threshold, god of the door, etc. Thus the Romans were very receptive to strange gods, on two conditions: that the cult not have an orgiastic character, and that the god not claim exclusive adoration. It was in this way that the Roman pantheon was enriched in the course of time. This is why Roman society always included a kind of religious *avant-garde*, receptive to novelty largely out of curiosity and a little out of snobbery.

Our great ladies belonged to this type. It is certain that ancient Roman religion was first extinguished in their families. Proof can be found in the slight interest they took in sacerdotal duties. In spite of the respect attached to their persons and the honors accorded to them, the vestal virgins were recruited with difficulty. The great families, when solicited, scarcely ever offered their daughters, and Augustus felt compelled to make a great declaration regretting that his family included no little girl of an age to fulfill the requirements. Under Tiberius, a sensational event took place and was remarked on as such: two children were placed in competition. The choice went to the worthier, the one whose parents had not been divorced, but the other was thanked and given magnificent gifts. To enhance even further the prestige of this office, Tiberius was delighted to send his mother into the vestals' box at the circus.

Meanwhile women participated, if only out of habit, in the ancient Roman cults to which Augustus attempted to restore a certain glamor. There was a whole series of official ceremonies which could not be avoided, and certain ones were reserved for matrons. On the first of March, for example, the *Matronalia*

76

were celebrated in honor of Juno Lucina and in commemoration of the reconciliation once effected by the Sabine women between their fathers and their husbands. The married women carried flowers and garlands to Juno, and a sacrifice was performed. The principle of these annual ceremonies may be found in the entirely Greek festival in Juno's honor which Ovid describes so beautifully:

> There stands an ancient sacred grove, all dark with shadows from dense trees; behold it – you would agree a deity indwelt the place. An altar receives the prayers and votive incense of the faithful – an artless altar, upbuilt by hands of old. From here, when the pipe has sounded forth in solemn strain, advances over carpeted ways the annual pomp; snowy heifers are led along mid the plaudits of the crowd, heifers reared

The traditional sacrifice: old Roman cults.

in their native meadows of Faliscan grass, and calves that threaten with brow not yet to be feared, and, lesser victim, a pig from the lowly sty, and the leader of the flock, with hard temples overhung by the curving horn. The she-goat only is hateful to the mistress-deity; through her tale-telling, they say, the goddess was found in the deep forest and made to cease the flight she had entered on .... Wherever the goddess will pass, youths and timid maidens go before, sweeping the broad ways with trailing robe. The maidens' locks are pressed by gold and gems, and the proud palla covers feet that are bright with gold; in the manner of their Grecian sires of yore, veiled in white vestments they bear on their heads the sacred offerings of old. The crowd keep reverent silence as the golden pomp comes on, with the goddess' self close in the wake of her ministers.

After the procession, the livestock was sacrificed before the temple.

To take part in great festivities was sometimes an actual honor: to be one of the choir of nine virgins from noble families who marched singing in groups of three ahead of the procession, to be included among the twenty-seven young girls who sang at the Secular Games or at the obsequies of Augustus – these, as Horace says, were memories to be recalled later on. 'I also, at the time that the century celebrated its birth, repeated a song beloved of the gods, faithful to the cadences of the inspired poet, Horace.'

Certain of these festivals were not exempt from violence, like that of the Good Goddess. This mystery was celebrated each year at the beginning of December, at night, in the house of a magistrate invested with the imperium and under the direction of the mistress of the house. Men were rigorously excluded from the house, and all paintings and sculptures representing them were covered. Caesar had to divorce his wife Pomponia as the result of the frightful scandal caused by the discovery of a man in her dwelling during the celebration of this mystery. Juvenal has left us a description of it which, as always, we must take to be distorted, and of which decency demands that we reproduce only an innocuous section: 'The secrets of Bona Dea are well known. When the pipe excites them, and inflamed alike with the horn and wine, these Maenads of Priapus rush wildly round, and whirl their locks and howl!'

In daily life the official cults maintained their power to the degree that they fell in with superstitious beliefs. Prayers were uttered for the beauty of daughters when passing a temple of Venus, offerings were made to the goddess of childbirth in the event of pregnancy. Great importance was attached to omens: when she was expecting Tiberius, Livia, wanting to know if she would bear a son, took an egg from under a sitting hen and reheated it until it hatched. The chick sported a fine crest! It was also Livia who, one day while visiting her property in Veii soon after her marriage to Augustus, saw an eagle drop a white hen which carried a laurel twig in its beak. The pious Livia had the chicken cared for and planted the twig. The hen had numerous progeny which caused the house to be surnamed 'of the hens.' As for the twig, it soon gave birth to a laurel grove. This laurel was used to crown the Caesars at their triumphs; but it was noticed that a tree died each time a Caesar died. The whole grove died with Nero!

The most violent manifestations of fervor came from the Oriental cults. There are many reasons for their success: their ceremonies were accompanied by pomp and complicated ritual; they were surrounded with mystery and struck the imagination. In short, these cults answered to a need for exaltation and mysticism; they introduced an asceticism which counterbalanced a somewhat lax morality.

It was among women that the Orient had the most success. Juvenal jeers at their excesses of piety:

> She will break the ice and plunge into the river in the depth of winter, or dip three times in Tiber at early dawn, and bathe her timid head in its very eddies, and thence emerging will crawl on bleeding knees, naked and shivering, over the whole field of the haughty king. If white Io command, she will go to the extremity of Egypt, and bring back water fetched from scorching Meroe, to sprinkle on the temple of Isis, that rears itself hard by the ancient sheepfold. For she believes that the warning is given her by the voice of the goddess herself.

The great goddess Isis, with a thousand names, was the one whom women most commonly invoked. They thronged her temples. Clothed in the required linen garments, they sang twice a day in honor of the goddess, they went to have themselves sprinkled with Nile water, and observed the fasts and prescriptions of abstinence imposed by the priests, among them the chastity required by certain festivals, which might last ten to thirty days! To transgress constituted a serious sin ... but for a good price, the priests would intercede with Osiris, and the sacrifice of a fat goose or a thin cake would appease the god. In addition, it must not be thought that this cult of Isis was pleasing to those in power. Augustus, victorious over Antony, had also conquered the East, and above all Egypt. And now an Egyptian god was all the rage in Rome! Augustus forbade the devotees of Isis to congregate within the sacred confines of the city, and then extended this interdict to within the radius of a mile around Rome. Meanwhile a temple of Isis and Serapis had been built on the Campus Martius. As the result of a scandal, Tiberius had it demolished in the year 19 A.D., had the image of the goddess cast into the river, and forbade the practice of the cult to Roman citizens. Nothing came of this: the persecution

ceased with Caligula, and the imperial family itself was chief among those faithful to Isis. The silver serpent and the Egyptian sistrum were part of Roman life from that time on.

One of Ovid's elegies shows quite well the ambiguous and nonselective character of the Roman cults. The poet fears for Corinna's life. In his despair he does not shrink from invoking all the gods who might help his mistress:

> O Isis, thou that lovest Paraetonium and Canopus' genial fields, Memphis, and Pharos rich in palms, and where swift Nile glides down and from his broad bed comes forth to the waters of the sea through seven mouths, by thy sistrums I beseech, by the face of revered Anubis – so may loyal Osiris ever love thy rites, and the sluggish serpent glide about thy altar-gifts, and horned Apis be thy comrade in the pomp! – turn hither thy countenance, and in one spare us both! For thou wilt give life to my lady, and she to me. Oft has she sat in ministration to thee on the days fixed for thy service, where the Gallic squadron rides near thy laurel-trees . . . . And thou who hast compassion for women in their pangs, when their heavy bodies are tense with the hidden load, do thou attend in mercy and give ear to my prayers, O Ilithyia! She is worthy of aid from thee – do thou bid her live! Myself in shining robes will offer incense on thy smoking altars, myself bring votive gifts and lay them at thy feet. I will add the legend: 'Naso, for Corinna saved!' Do thou but give occasion for the legend and the gifts.

Isis, the new goddess, and Ilithyia Lucina, the ancient Latin goddess, seem to have got on well together!

The devout were easy to persuade, and the priests were suspected of promoting all kinds of infamy. A scandal, embarrassing at the very least, broke out under the principate of Tiberius. A great lady named Paulina, deeply devoted to Isis, and of irreproachable chastity, had been pursued by the attentions of a knight, Decius Mundus. For five hundred denarii the despairing suitor bought the priests of the temple where she was in the habit of going. They made her believe that the god Anubis wished an interview with her during the night. It was Mundus, of course, who appeared in the mask of Anubis!

This story unfortunately does not appear to be the only one of its kind. Propertius, Ovid, and Juvenal echo each other in

83

accusing the temples of frequently transforming themselves into places of assignation, with the priests and priestesses as go-betweens.

Instead of performing their devotions, our great ladies might also attend the judicial debates in the Forum; certain ladies were constantly in the audience. But most preferred to go to public readings. This amusement had become one of the favorite pastimes of good society, since the Romans, deprived of politics, could thereafter become excited only about the literary profession. Poetry was more than ever in vogue. Tacitus claimed that the poet was less exposed than the orator to the danger of giving offense. Hearing the spoken word seemed an advantage entirely different from reading a book, and rather than listen to a slave read aloud, people preferred to gather together in company around a poet. To this amusement was added the pleasure of keeping up with the latest novelty. For the authors it was an opportunity to present their works to a circle of connoisseurs who were ready to applaud. The itch to lose no time occasionally led to imprudence: a knight, C. Lutorius Priscus, had composed an elegy on the occasion of Germanicus' death which fetched him a reward from Tiberius. In 21 A.D., when Tiberius' son Drusus fell seriously ill, our man hastened to compose an elegy on the death of Drusus; his vanity egged him on, and he gave a reading of it to a large circle of highborn ladies. Denounced by the senate, he was condemned for the crime of *lèse-majesté*, and paid for his anticipation with his life.

The ordinary day of our Roman lady has a delightful conclusion in the evening banquet. In fact this meal played an important part in social life. The literature of the time abounds in stories of importunate hangers-on who came to beg the privilege of dining at their patron's table. Here, too, the imperial family set the tone, and all Rome would conceive a passion for a root that Julia was fond of. In the matter of receptions, if Augustus and Tiberius liked simple meals (three courses, and a limited number of guests chosen for their intelligence), Caligula and Claudius liked great banquets. The latter would invite up to six hundred people in a carefully chosen setting. Finally, it was proper to mark certain unusual occasions: for example, when Tiberius returned triumphantly to Rome, victorious over the Pannonians and the Dalmatians, Augustus gave a banquet in his honor to the men, while Livia and Julia were giving one for the women.

84

The main meal of the Romans to which guests were invited was the *cena*, or dinner, which came at the beginning of the evening after the bath. Its length varied with its importance. Decency required the meal to be finished at nightfall, but in fact the banquets were prolonged well into the night, sometimes even until dawn.

Banquets multiplied opportunities for debauchery. The chief one arose from the custom of eating stretched out on beds. This habit, at first reserved for the gods, was adopted by men, and then by women. Only children were seated on stools. In the most simple arrangement, three sloping beds were grouped around a table. On each bed cushions marked out three places, and their distribution depended on a complicated etiquette. The guests lay sideways, the left elbow resting on a cushion, the feet on the lower part of the couch. What fortunate arrangements, and how pleasant it was to take advantage of them by the dim light of the torches! Ovid says:

Bread and circuses . . .
Nero and Poppaea in "The Sign of the Cross".

Banquets too give openings, when the tables are set; something other than wine may you find there. Often has bright-hued Love with soft arms drawn to him and embraced the horns of Bacchus as he there reclined . . . . Wine gives courage and makes men apt for passion . . . . At such time often have women bewitched the minds of men, and Venus in the wine has been fire in fire. Trust not at such a time o'ermuch to the treacherous lamp; darkness and drink impair your judgment of beauty . . . that hour makes any woman fair.

For women, he is lavish with advice: 'Come late, and make a graceful entrance when the lamp has been set: delay will enhance your charm: delay is a great procuress. Though plain, to the tipsy you will seem fair; and night herself will hide your faults.' And then what happened, when a woman took her place on a bed next to a possible suitor? Both must pray to Bacchus, whose rites are celebrated at night, to keep from their heads the noxious fumes of the wine. At that point the man could address to his lady a tender speech in veiled terms, whose meaning she would have no trouble understanding.

. . . you may trace light flatteries in thin characters of wine, that on the table she may read herself your mistress; you may gaze at her eyes with eyes that confess their flame: there are often voice and words in a silent look. See that you are the first to seize the cup her lips have touched, and drink at that part where she has drunk; and whatever food she has touched with her fingers see that you ask for, and while you ask contrive to touch her hand. Let it also be your aim to please your lady's husband; he is often more useful to you, if made a friend. To him, if you drink by lot, concede the first turn; give him the garland tossed from your own head. Whether he be below you or hold an equal place, let him take of all before you; nor hesitate to yield him place in talk . . . As real drunkenness does harm, so will feigned bring profit: make your crafty tongue stumble in stammering talk, so that, whatever you do or say more freely than you should, may be put down to too much wine . . . It is better not to drink too much: drunkenness arouses a man's disgust. As for the woman, in that state she deserves to be delivered up to the first comer.

Nevertheless, it seems that other liberties were taken besides those recommended by Ovid for conquering a beauty. In another text, the poet does not hide his pain at the thought that his mistress' husband must attend the banquet that evening. But the experience is worth the torment. And so we will be less hard on Augustus, who took a consul's wife away from the table before her husband's eyes and only brought her back some time later, flushed and disheveled.

This conduct is at least in part explained by the way in which the meal progressed. A great deal was eaten and drunk, the dishes were quite varied and served in many courses. Women particularly enjoyed mushrooms, truffles, liver paste, suckling pig roasted on a spit, and lettuce. Olives accompanied the entire meal. The art of Roman cooking lay in the serving of the dishes, in arranging them in such a way that the guests should not know exactly what they were eating. Martial proposes a simple kind of menu:

> My steward has brought me some laxative mallows, and the various riches with which my garden is adorned – flat lettuce and a leek for cutting into slices, not forgetting the pleasant mint nor the cabbage which awakens love. Finely chopped eggs will surmount the anchovies on a bed of rue, and there will be sow's udders spiced with pickled tuna. After that my modest repast will only admit of one single course: a kid snatched from the teeth of the fierce wolf, grilled cutlets, beans and young green cabbages. To this will be added a chicken and a ham which has already survived three meals. When you are no longer hungry, I will serve you ripe fruits and a flagon of Nomentum without the lees.

The true banquet had seven courses: appetizers, three entrees, two roasts, and dessert. It is understandable that Ovid advises young women, his pupils in the art of pleasing, not to seem to throw themselves on the food: in any case, they did not risk dying of hunger!

By contrast, 'A young woman may decently allow herself a certain excess in drinking,' provided that she preserves her lucidity. There was no lack of opportunities to drink: a first libation before the meal, a honeyed wine after the appetizer, and various wines between the other courses. The wine came out of amphoras in which it had been preserved in resin and pitch; and so it was poured into a bowl through a strainer in order to filter it. Water was added to it, either chilled with snow or heated, according to the wine, and then the cups had only to draw off the precious liquid. The feast sometimes ended with a drinking bout in which a whole series of cups was emptied at one draught, their number and the way of emptying them being specified by the president of the banquet.

Heads and stomachs have difficulty withstanding so much food and drink: our guests, who were insatiable gluttons, readily made use of emetics – for health's sake, of course.

The atmosphere of the gathering was enhanced by entertainment, an obligatory accompaniment to the simplest of meals. Various distractions were offered between dishes, and also while the guests were eating. Performers, mountebanks, popular circus pantomimists, and more often clowns came to go through their acts, or even perform a comedy or give a reading – from the works of the master or mistress of the house; or they declaimed poems, which was highly respectable. But the most usual entertainment, which was also a part of all those just mentioned, was

music. Our contemporaries did not invent 'dinner music.' The concert-banquet was the rage; licentious songs would certainly be sung, and also one could admire the melodies and voluptuous dances of Andalusia and Gades. All this combined to affront the ears, eyes, or modesty of the ladies – but it provided an uninterrupted musical background for the whole dinner.

The guests were entertained, but they were ready to entertain themselves; they lent themselves to the general mood by interpreting songs, or taking a part in them themselves, like the young lady advised by Ovid to 'abandon her cup and move her arms in rhythm to the sound of the instruments.' Finally, the host had the task of giving his guests the opportunity to discourse on familiar and agreeable subjects. The Romans were a chatty people, and it would not have done to deprive them of that great pleasure – the art of conversation. Ladies took part in it brilliantly; their specialty seems to have been literary criticism. According to Juvenal, nothing was more annoying than those women who began to discuss literature as soon as they were at table with such a lot of noise that no one, not even another woman, felt capable of stopping them.

But aside from ordinary days, there were more festive ones. In contempt of daily routine, when the Games were given everyone went off to the arena from morning until evening. The circus was the choice amusement, and women attended as well as men. Everyone knows the important role of the Games in Roman society; they constituted the surest means of capturing the favor of the crowd. Under the empire, they took the place of the political activity of the republic. At the arena, popularity was manifested and judged by greetings and acclamations. There, contact was established with the sovereign, petitions were presented. Emperors vied in ostentatious and magnificent organization of the Games, and they made it their duty to attend in person. Sometimes a banquet was even given, and everyone partook of it without distinction of age, class, or sex.

The spectacles held an extraordinary place in Roman life, and this was true in all classes of society. Everyone went before dawn to secure his seats. On the holidays a special police force watched over the deserted city, which was the easy prey of thieves. These spectacles were a part of life because of their frequency; at the beginning of the empire the year included sixty-six days dedicated to Games, to which special Games were added each year. The number of these increased under each emperor: birthdays of

The amphitheater at Pompeii.

sovereigns, certain triumphs, commemorations. Under Tiberius one can count eighty-seven special holidays, but it quickly becomes impossible to establish an accurate list.

The ladies rivaled each other in elegance: one went to the arena to see, but also to be seen. What expense will a beauty not incur in order to go to the theater? If funds were low, '. . . that she may go in due state to the games, she hires a dress, and attendants, and a sedan, and pillow, and female friends, and a nurse, and yellow-haired girl to whom she may issue her commands.' It was necessary to 'make an appearance' at any cost; and this was all the more natural since men were required to come in 'full dress' – that is, wearing a toga.

Women, however, did not always enjoy the same prerogatives. Augustus decided that at the theater and amphitheater, men and women should sit in different places. The upper tiers were reserved for the female sex. This moral precaution explains the attitude which the seducer had to adopt at the theater:

. . . nor let her sit in the round theater, her fair looks by you unheeded: something worth looking at she will bring on her shoulders. On her you may turn your looks, her you may

admire: much let your eyebrows, much let your gestures say.
Applaud when an actor portrays some woman in his dance,
and favor whoever be the lover that is played. When she
rises you will rise; while she sits you will sit too ...

Nevertheless, it was not very convenient for making advances.
For that purpose, the circus was the ideal place, since there
men and women were mixed. The expert Ovid asserts:

   ... the spacious circus holds many opportunities. No need
is there of fingers for secret speech, nor need you receive a
signal by means of nods. Sit next to your lady, none will
prevent you; sit side by side as close as you can; and that is
easy, for the rows compel closeness, if she be unwilling, and
by the rule of the place you must touch your comrade. Here
seek an opening for friendly talk, and begin with words that
all may hear. Mind you are zealous in asking whose horses
are entering, and quick! whomsoever she favors be sure to
favor too .... And if perchance, as will happen, a speck of
dust falls on your lady's lap, then flick it off with your fingers;
and if none fall, then flick off – none; let any pretext serve

your turn. If her cloak hangs low and trails upon the ground, gather it up and lift it carefully from the defiling earth; straightway, a reward for your service, with the girl's permission your eyes will catch a glimpse of her ankles. Then again look round to see that whoever is sitting behind you is not pressing his knee against her tender back. Frivolous minds are won by trifles: many have found useful the deft arranging of a cushion. It has helped too to stir the air with a light fan, or to set a stool beneath a dainty foot ... Such openings will the circus afford to a new courtship ...

One anecdote illustrates rather well both the atmosphere of the circus and that of the imperial family: Julia, exquisitely dressed, used to appear at the circus surrounded by a swarm of frivolous young men. Augustus, who reproached her, recommending the example of Livia, who was soberly dressed and accompanied by men of age and substance, provoked this reply: 'These will grow old with me!'

'Innocent modesty is destroyed at the theater.' Is this true? Or should it rather be thought that the theater was only a place of perdition for women if they wanted it to be? In reality, the pernicious influence which everyone recognized in it issued from another cause: it came from the very nature of the representations. To be sure, at the circus the chariot races only excited the emotions of the spectators, but what about the Games in the amphitheater? Gladiators fought with animals, to the death; on the pretext of mythological representations, condemned criminals were put to death under the most frightful tortures. All this bloodshed perhaps explains, without excusing, the contempt women felt for human life outside the common law – slaves or criminals. 'A slave on the cross? What does it matter?' It was not a man.

The theater itself attacked morality. Dramatic representations were not costly to put on, hence their frequency. There was nothing intellectual in this theater, which most often only amounted to Atellan farce, mime, and pantomime. The Atellan was a popular farce of crude comedy, which teemed with raw jokes. As for mime, it was character comedy dealing with vulgar subjects: fraud, chicanery and above all adultery. The surprised lover lets himself be carried away in a clothespress to escape the wrath of the cuckolded husband, the husband sends his pretty wife to a powerful enemy whom he fears, so that she will disarm him with her attractions. The female parts were played by women, and at the request of the public they embellished their roles with a number of dances. Pantomime, finally, was very fashionable. It appeared under the reign of Augustus and to a considerable degree replaced tragedy, which was dying out. The most important moments of action consisted of a suite of lyric solos executed by a single actor, who played several parts in succession while the text was sung by a choir accompanied by an orchestra. The subjects, borrowed chiefly from Greek mythology, were enjoyed all the more for being indecent. The mime, a universal being, able to play all the parts, to sing, and especially to dance, had to possess incomparable beauty. He maintained it by strict care and discipline, worthy of our modern stars.

A soothsayer is not needed to predict the consequences of this state of things: the passion of both men and women for these performers. Scandalous stories abounded, for the actors lived on the fringes of society. They were not free men, but that did not matter; they aroused the most insane passions. 'Urbicus provokes a laugh by his personification of Autonoe in the Atellan farce. Aelia, being poor, is in love with him. For others, the comic actor unbuckles his garment for a large sum.' Others ruined Chrysogonus. Hispulla was infatuated with a tragedian.

Hippia, though wife to a senator, accompanied a gladiator to Pharos and the Nile, and the infamous walls of Lagos . . . And yet what was the beauty that inflamed, what the prime of life that captivated Hippia? What was it she saw in him to compensate for being nicknamed the fencer's whore? For the darling Sergius had now begun to shave his throat; and, badly wounded in the arm, to anticipate his discharge. Besides, he had many things to disfigure his face, as for instance – he was galled with his helmet, and had a huge wen between his nostrils, and acrid rheum forever trickling from his eye. But then he was a gladiator! It is this that makes them beautiful as Hyacinthus!

It is a sorry picture which Juvenal draws here, but this gladiator story does not seem to have been the only one of its kind, although it is extreme. Under the reign of Augustus one young wife had her head shaved in order to follow, disguised as a servant boy, the comedian Stephanion, who as a result of this affair was beaten with rods in Rome's three theaters and banished by order of Augustus. The proprieties were not to be trifled with! But this kind of punishment prevented nothing. At the beginning of Tiberius' reign, in 15 A.D. and then in 22 and 23, measures were taken against actors. In 15 a limit was put on their wages, senators were forbidden to frequent pantomimists, knights were forbidden to accompany them in the street. In 22 or 23 such a disturbance arose about them that it came to the point of their banishment from Italy. But none of it lasted. Men and women were proud to walk besides mimes in the street, to appear to be their servants.

Ladies seized on the favors of actors, particularly the mimes, who became the prey of the imperial family. Caligula nursed a passion which lived after him for the handsome Mnester, who in another connection had an understanding with the prettiest woman of the day, one Poppaea, the wife of a senator. Messalina, deeply jealous of this Poppaea, contrived to ruin her and finally drove her to suicide. Mnester then became the Empress' lover – under orders and by coercion, he later declared! Messalina nevertheless seems to have been much attached to him. She kept him away from the theater and had statues cast in gold in his honor: but Mnester was condemned to death along with Messalina's other lovers or accomplices, an expiatory victim of the splendor and slavery of the Roman actor's life.

Such was the attraction of the Games that ladies were reluctant to leave Rome and be bored in the country. But all rules have their exceptions, and certain resorts by the sea offered agreeable compensations.

The unhealthiness of Rome in summer and early autumn, the harshness of some winters, the fatigue provoked by noise and urban living stimulated the Romans, from the republican period on, to take vacations. This taste had spread to such a degree that important people possessed a choice of villas diversely situated in the country, by the sea, or in the mountains. The number of these houses was so large, even among relatively modest people like Cicero or Pliny, that they eventually could serve as stopping places on the stages of long journeys. They were possessions that could easily be disposed of; they were sold and others were bought elsewhere. This gave opportunities for redecoration and for taking vacations in different places. The multiplication of these residences in Italy caused Horace to fear a total disappearance of the cultivation of vineyards and olive

groves, there was such an invasion of buildings, artificial lakes, myrtle or laurel thickets, violet beds. Houses were squeezed together along the coast. They formed an actual rampart around Ostia, Antium, Formii, and especially around the bay of Naples. To have one house in the Alban or Sabine hills near Rome, for breathing pure air – that was all right; one other near a lake in the north of Italy was also nice; but a villa by the sea was indispensable. The lack of land, and the desire peculiar to Romans for conquering difficulties necessitated audacity in construction: on a rock, inside a rock, and even on the water, the houses appeared wherever the owner's whim dictated. Under the sea around Antium exist the remains of these houses which had been built on terrain created out of nothing. 'Everywhere the sea forms a bay, you immediately place foundations and create an artificial earth,' remarks Seneca. It was to Campania, in particular to the Gulf of Naples, and especially to Baiae that all Rome hurried in the summer months. The imperial family was to be found there, and this small locality was undoubtedly the most frequented seaside town, the most luxurious pleasure city of antiquity. The town was right on the beach inside a border of mountains. It included convalescent homes and numerous buildings for the amusement of guests in good health. People used to go to Baiae to take the waters, but they went especially to enjoy life with complacency. They relished the charm of the South, and of constantly renewed festivities. The indolence and license of life there were proverbial. Feasts and pleasure parties succeeded one another on the shore and on innumerable barks and gondolas. Music and singing resounded from morning until evening and sometimes far into the night. Need it be said that Baiae was one of the favorite places of great Roman ladies? A very dangerous spot, though, since more than one 'arrived there with the air of Penelope and left like another Helen!'

Rome and Italy thus offered a woman all fashionable possibilities, but in our period she was no longer satisfied with Italy and Rome . . . .

Cape Misenum.

Travel

. . . It is not without reason that it used to be forbidden to take women along, either among allies or into foreign countries; the company of women has the effect of encumbering peacetime with luxuriousness, and wartime with fears; they give a Roman army on the march the aspect of a barbarian horde. Their sex is not only weak and unused to fatigue, but if left to itself it is also cruel, ambitious, and eager for authority. They come among the soldiers and arrange the places of the centurions. Lately, a woman presided over the drilling of the cohorts and over the parading of the legions . . . . The Senate should bear in mind it is against wives that the most serious charges are brought in all cases of bribery, it is to them that the most discredited provincials first attach themselves, it is they who take affairs in hand and they who manage them. Because of them two escorts are necessary, two general headquarters. Their wishes, more stubborn and more foolish, and once kept in check by the Oppian law and by other legislative provisions, now rule (since those fetters are broken) over families, tribunals, armies . . . .

This vehement indictment, which smacks of the old Roman misogynist, was pronounced to the senate in the year 20 A.D. by Caecina Severus. It establishes a fact of great importance: that women had begun to follow their husbands on journeys of long duration.

Under the republic one never heard of women in the country outside Roman territory. As a rule, they did not accompany their husbands; but the latter's journeys did not last very long. Starting with the principate, as a result of the extension of the Roman world the situation changed. From then on, there were professional soldiers, men who took service for twenty years. The Roman armies bordered the frontiers of an immense world which stretched from the plateaus of Asia Minor to the Atlantic, and from the Sahara to the North Sea. These armies fought or not, according to circumstances, but they stayed there. Soldiers and officers lived far away from Rome; for leaders as well as men, this situation might last a long time.

The civil wars at the end of the republic, on the other hand, had created the custom of traveling around the Mediterranean basin to escape this or that proscription. Then women took part in the activity: one of Mark Antony's wives, Fulvia, although remaining in Italy, gave proof of military activity by raising troops. However, she seemed to be an exception. But Cornelia accompanied her husband Pompey the Great across the sea to Egypt, where they expected to find refuge. Watching Pompey's ship from the top of her own vessel, she was a powerless and terrified witness to his assassination. Livia, then married to Tiberius Nero, who had fought against Octavius in Campania, made a dramatic escape after the latter's victory. Holding the infant Tiberius close to her bosom, taking out-of-the-way roads to avoid the troops, escorted by only one man in order to be better disguised, she finally reached Naples, where she embarked for Sicily. Then she went to Greece and established herself at Sparta, a city under the protection of her husband's family. The most interesting part of the story is that on her return she married the man from whom she had fled . . . .

Under the principate, we are no longer in such heroic times. In Roman society the imperial family played a part of official presence and representation. Although the emperors were not all such great travelers as Augustus, all wellborn young men pursued what might be called a colonial career. They were sent to head the legions of Germania, Pannonia, Dalmatia, or the East. Sometimes they met their death there, like Livia's son Drusus the first, or Caius, the son of Julia. Besides their military command, they might be called upon to govern one region or inspect another. These men traveled all over the Roman world without respite. Occasionally they established themselves for a certain length of time in a far-off province.

Germanicus' career, brutally cut short at the age of thirty-four, serves as an example. Immediately after his marriage to Agrippina the Elder under Augustus' reign, while still very young he went to Dalmatia and Pannonia under Tiberius' orders in 7 A.D. and in 9. In the year 11 he went to Germania. He returned to Rome a year later to take a consulship. Then he left again at the end of a year as governor of Germania, at the head of the eight legions of the Rhine. He spent five years there, in the course of which Augustus died. After another year's sojourn in Rome, he left again, armed with special powers for a tour of inspection in the provinces cut off by sea. He died in the course of his journey.

This example, chosen from many others, shows to what degree travel was involved in the life of the imperial family. The importance and length of the journeys depended on different reasons, one as cogent as another. On the one hand, it scarcely seemed politic to stay in Rome. If one was emperor – Augustus had provided the example – one risked getting oneself hated by punishing disobedient citizens, and if one pardoned them, one transgressed one's own laws. In every way one was obliged to display too much authority. In Rome, there were all kinds of traps set for members of the imperial family; it was necessary to preserve a constantly unstable equilibrium between the emperor's personal feelings, over which one could not show too much influence, and the often noisy manifestations of the senate and the Roman people, who were always ready to show sympathy or hostility. Life in Rome could be arduous, with its multiple intrigues, its atmosphere laden with suspicion, its 'old Roman' conformism preached by the government. One may judge from this: Germanicus – again – and his adoptive brother Drusus in the course of one of their official duties found themselves forbidden by the Emperor to speak in the senate. Their ties of relationship with the prince would have caused people to suppose that they expressed the official opinion.

To live in Rome then was not desirable. And the vast empire required generals at the frontiers and administrators in the provinces. The administration, the army, and especially the imperial presence constituted the bonds which united peoples as diverse as Germans, Gauls, Spaniards, Greeks, Asiatics, Syrians, Egyptians, and Africans. The emperor's visits, or those of members of his family, revived the loyalty of distant territories and gave further proof of Roman power.

So as not to be condemned to a life of semi-widowhood, the

women also got into the habit of leaving. The example came from a high place: Livia herself almost always accompanied her husband when he traveled. That, indeed, is what Tiberius' son Drusus replied to the discourse of Caecina Severus cited above. Antonia the Younger, Julia, the elder Agrippina, and Livilla are the best known of the imperial princesses who adopted this attitude, but the fashion caught on in all the great families. The antifeminist reaction of Tiberius' reign did not succeed in conquering it, since administrators lived a still longer time away from Rome than members of the imperial family: Tiberius, very conservative by inclination, left one of his favorites in Mesia for twenty years; Seneca's uncle stayed sixteen years as prefect of Egypt; and Pontius Pilate ten years as procurator of Judaea. It was impossible to forbid these men to take their wives with them.

A taste for travel itself was added to these political and administrative reasons. Tourism became fashionable among the Romans: whether the excuse was religion, health, education, or pleasure, people went on journeys.

The great religious ceremonies and their holiday processions made a good pretext. One could go from sanctuary to sanctuary getting initiated into secret cults. In this sphere the Romans were especially attracted by the Eleusinian mysteries. Traveling for the health also appeared under many guises. Certain of these journeys had a religious aspect, like visits to the great gods of healing: Aesculapius, Isis, Serapis. Therapeutic establishments were attached to their sanctuaries. Epidaurus in Greece, one of the most celebrated resorts, was still growing in the Roman epoch. Otherwise, fashions did not really change; people 'took the waters' at Baiae, Canopus, Aix-les-Bains, Bath. Certain of these resorts also soon became known as pleasure spots. Finally, the indispensable prescription for chest ailments was a change of air: so doctors sent their rich patients to Egypt or into pine forests, or perhaps to take a milk cure in the mountains. Without having to be ill, a short cruise along the Italian or Sicilian coast, or any trip whatsoever was always recommended in summer or winter, when people went to get the sun at Tarentum or Syracuse. This brings us to the last aspect of tourism: pleasure.

Traveling for pleasure – as one learns every year from travel-agency folders – may be conceived of in various ways according to individual taste. One might almost define the Romans by their notion of tourism. What interested them first of all was well

known things, even very well known. They were hardly tempted
at all by the unexpected or the original. They never even seemed
to depart from well trodden paths: they went in search of historical and mythological landmarks. This fits in very well with
their temperament as a people mindful of an honorable past.
And so they went to visit 'historic' places: the place where Cicero

was murdered, Augustus' birthplace, the lands of Greek legend – and they went to visit temples.

Temples, in fact, were actually repositories. The word 'museum' evokes the notion of classification, which was certainly not the point here. By virtue of offerings, legacies, or deposits, all kinds of objects were accumulated there which formed a strange gallery of curiosities – the kind of thing that in the eighteenth century came to be called an 'amateur collection.' And so, on the one hand, works of art might be found there – paintings and sculptures, cameos and vases, but also a huge piece of crystal – Livia's offering to the Capital – or a suit of armor set with pearls from Brittany, offered by Caesar to the temple of Mother Venus, or elephants' tusks, and objects of historical interest like Caesar's sword, Colycrates' ring, the linen cuirass of King Amasis, etc. Some of these were actual relics, although of course often false: Leda's egg; a cup offered by Helen, the exact cast of her breast; the ships of Agamemnon, Aeneas, Ulysses . . . . Naturally, the priests and servants attached to the temples were in charge of explanations. In the cities, chiefly in Greece, there were even guides, called *periegetes,* who were responsible for conducting visitors. 'Everywhere, one only hears tell of what once existed,' stated the rhetorician Aristides.

The present interested no one. The sense of the picturesque, to which the modern world pays so much attention, was unknown. This is particularly noticeable in the Roman's love of nature, the other motive for their travels. 'Among all the things which uplift the spirit and bring us pleasure,' says Atticus, 'the palm goes to nature.' But it was not a question of the grandeur of a landscape, or the sentiments which its contemplation might produce; the essential thing was to experience religious feeling, to enter more easily into contact with the gods:

When you see a sacred wood with ancient trees growing close together to their full height, whose bushy mass of interlaced branches masks the celestial vault, the spectacular growth of vegetation, the mystery of the place, the wonderful and potent shadows cast on the plain cause you to feel as if in the presence of a divinity. In the same way when you see a grotto where the stone is eroded by time, which has made a deep pit in the side of a mountain, and when you have established that this excavation is not artificial but is entirely the effect of natural causes, this sight will fill your soul with the sense of the existence of a higher power. We worship the sources of great rivers; there altars are raised, where the impetuous flood escapes from the chasm which hid it from our eyes; hot springs have their cult; and more than one lake is reputed holy, because of its dark color or the soundless depths of its waters.

The sacred character of a place was an attraction. To go and visit trees is a concept evidently quite foreign to our minds, but it does occur to us to look at landscapes because they have been celebrated in literature. This was a common thing in Rome. People were also interested in natural phenomena that seemed unusual: movements of the tide, sulphur springs.

Finally, but much less so than in our time, it happened that Romans were drawn by the sheer beauty of a place. They liked scenery with water and foliage, restful, calm, and cool. The spectacular, the sublime, the wild, all these romantic conceptions of nature were not in vogue: and the Alps, though constantly being crossed, were only associated with terror and with difficulties which it gave no one pleasure to overcome. Nevertheless, it remains true that their taste for nature and for the past gave our Roman men and women more reason to travel.

After distinguishing between tourism and long journeys of administrative character, the extent of the Roman Empire allowed two very different kinds of trip: Eastern or Western. A Western journey did not offer the inducements of an Eastern one, nor from such a distance. In Germania, battles were incessant and had uncertain results. The dark forests, the cold and misty climate of that country bewildered the Romans, who found the atmosphere hostile. Love, such as Agrippina's for Germanicus, was needed for a woman to agree to settle near the camp. In spite of the slaves, life with the armies lacked comfort. It could be heroic. Most of the time the ladies preferred to settle down in Narbon Gaul, at the most Romanized places which recalled something of Italy, like Nimes, for instance. If need be, they would go as far as Lyons.

Roadways were used to get to these regions. Created for reasons of strategy, the Roman roads had been developed in proportion to the conquests. At the beginning of the empire, the Roman system of roadways was remarkable for its extensiveness and relative density. It was also outstanding in the quality of its stone-paved surfaces, some of which have been preserved until the present day, both on flat country and in the

hills. Detailed signs were placed to indicate stops, the direction of the roads, distances, and spots where a resting place could be found for the night. Some of these were actual guides, containing in addition some indication of the curiosities to be seen, with historical notes.

It must seldom have been the fashion for these women – or even for their husbands – to travel modestly on foot, on muleback, or in any rented carriage. Simplicity only suited such men as Horace, who charmingly recounts a trip he made to Brundusium. His example shows us what an ordinary journey was: the traveler went on foot, in a boat, or in a vehicle, taking what he found from one stopping place to another. As for resting places, they were extremely varied, from an inn where the serving maid did wonders, to the house of an absent friend, besides one

night spent on board ship: all in all he spent twelve days going from Rome to Brundusium.

A Roman lady of a certain rank did not travel without taking along servants, slaves, friends, and a mass of luggage which would assure her everywhere of maximum comfort and her habitual luxurious surroundings. Gold and silver dishes and a set of furniture were only normal accessories; everyone had favorite objects among his personal treasures which he was never without. Already under the republic Caesar never traveled without his mosaic floors, Antony without his collection of gold vases. And so carriage followed carriage until a regular caravan was formed which had to be preceded by slaves responsible for clearing the way. One can imagine the style of these expeditions when one learns that it was chic to entrust this job to Negroes dressed in gaudy costumes. Nero and Poppaea undoubtedly furnish an extreme case: the Emperor never left without taking at least a thousand carriages drawn by mules fitted out in silver, which were led by muleteers dressed in red wool from Canusium and accompanied by a multitude of footmen and runners covered with bracelets and ornaments. As for Poppaea, her name has come down in history thanks to the five hundred she-asses that provided her daily milk bath and without which she never moved.

The display of luxury for which these journeys gave an opportunity, the glittering liveries of the slaves, the embroidered and decorated saddle covers of the horses and mules, the beauty of the carriages – this display of luxury was such that for many traveling ladies, true opulence only appeared on the highway. It is easy to understand the desire for refinements in the carriages themselves. They had to provide relative comfort for reading, writing, and sleeping, in a pleasant setting among gold and silver ornaments and curtains of costly materials. In some cases, however, ladies preferred litters, in which they reclined at their ease and gossiped.

Journeys were long, even without so much luggage. Couriers on horseback traveled thirty-five miles a day on the average; the mail carriages, borrowed by officials who were in a great hurry, could make around four-and-a-half miles an hour including stops, but this was exceptional. Stops were made for eating, resting, changing horses. Horace spent twelve days making the journey of 330 miles from Rome to Brundusium; going somewhat faster, it was done in a bit less than ten days, which is a little more than thirty-three miles a day.

Many of these personages, with their whole train, would occasionally sleep in tents or have themselves put up by town officials; but if one of their friends had a house near by, they would establish themselves there, even in the owner's absence.

There were inns everywhere, in towns, at crossroads or even along the road, which sometimes gave its name to the taverns beside it. Hostelries attracted the patron with publicity – good service, baths, and facilities 'in the fashion of the capital.' It seems that there was a relative choice. But hotels had a bad reputation except at large resorts. They were filled with smoke, uproar, bad smells, and bad company. Lice were numerous. Inns were often houses of prostitution, and travelers were cheated with watered wine and ill-fed animals. The law had to come to the aid of travelers, and innkeepers became responsible for the damages suffered by their customers during their stay.

The journey eastward which took the Romans all the way around the Mediterranean was undoubtedly more interesting. Here is Pliny:

> There are many curious things in Rome and in the environs of the capital which have never been seen and which are known only through hearsay. There would be many more chances of knowing them, through books, accounts of other

The hotels had an evil reputation.

people, or by having seen them personally, if they had been offered by Greece, Asia Minor, Egypt, or some other country rich in curiosities and understanding of their value.

The Eastern journey was a thrilling tour through countries with a climate like that of southern Italy, in the midst of wealth and interesting landmarks. For people who doted on literary and historical souvenirs, Greece and Asia were true places of pilgrimage, where each step raised the dust of the past.

Greece was the most accessible country. Every cultivated Roman owed it to himself to go there at least once in his life. People visited Athens, Corinth, Epidaurus and the sanctuary of Aesculapius, and Rhodes, the most flourishing island in Greece. Asia Minor was less easy to reach, but a good Roman could not dispense with a pilgrimage to Ilion on the site of Ancient Troy, the cradle of Aeneas. The inhabitants of this small town – wretched in the Greek period, and turned by the Romans into a relatively important little city – told how Trojan refugees had come back to their country after the Greeks had left, and rebuilt a city. Alexander the Great had come to Ilion to be shown Paris' lyre and the armor of Homer's heroes. In actuality, a learned controversy arose over the merits of this identification of Ilion with Troy, but besides the fact that it could appear to be the issue of jealous minds, it did not get beyond a small circle of scholars. And so people went on visiting the temple and the place where Pallas' image had been, although it had since been transferred to Rome.

As for foreign and mysterious Egypt, to which Augustus had forbidden access for senators and knights without authorization, it was the one region within the Roman world which provided the most total removal from familiar surroundings. Its civilization, impervious to Roman influence, made it a strange land of irresistible allure, and it was taken up by fashion particularly in the realm of art. The Nile with its mystery, the flora and fauna, became the theme of landscape painting and mosaics. People had always gone to see the same places ever since the first Greek travelers in the sixth century b.c.: Alexandria, Canopus, the Pyramids, Thebes and the Colossus of Memnon, the first cataract. Testimony of these visits has remained engraved on the stone, since many travelers wanted to immortalize themselves by leaving traces along the way!

Travel was carried on by ship in the summer months, because

112

except in serious cases – exile, flight, or the transfer of a prisoner – navigation stopped between November and March. Conditions on these maritime voyages are not in fact well known. Representations of ships in sculpture or mosaic seem to have been so fanciful that up to now it has been impossible to reconstruct a navigable ship from these data. Texts are also lacking, and the newest of archeologies, underwater archeology, has come to the aid of scholars. Sunken ships have been recovered, and these remains, well preserved in the mud, at least give an idea of the dimensions of merchant ships: around forty-four yards in length and around eleven in width. The cargo of these vessels was limited to around two thousand amphoras, although they could

hold much more. The ancients make reference to huge ships like the one built in Augustus' time for bringing an obelisk to Rome, which also carried 1,200 passengers and a load of papyrus, linen, and grain. Certain of these ships, called 'rounds,' specialized in transporting grain or horses. They navigated under sail. A cabin was fitted up on the poop for the commander and for people allowed near him, and along the deck were other cabins, sometimes very luxurious, with bathrooms. The sails were of various colors: black was a sign of mourning, red was reserved for the admiral's or the emperor's ship. Lanterns were lit at night and the ship often continued on its course. We have some idea of the length of these sea voyages. From Pozzuoli to Alexandria, the traditional route between Italy and Egypt, the crossing took twelve days on the average, but according to Pliny, the record was nine days. With a very favorable wind, it took five days from Pozzuoli to Corinth. The isthmus was crossed by hauling the vessel over a wooden track; but ships often went around the Peloponnesus.

Whether he traveled by sea or by land it was normal for a 'grandee' to depart accompanied by his wife, friends, and household. When Tiberius retired to Rhodes in Augustus' time, the fact that he left without his wife and friends was remarked on as unusual. It was a sign of his conjugal and political disgrace.

But women did not always follow their husbands. Certain places lent themselves particularly to long residence: Athens, where Octavia went in vain to wait for Antony, and Mitylene, on the island of Lesbos, where Julia spent the winter while Agrippa was on the continent. Julia even went on her own journeys as a tourist. She visited the island of Samos, celebrated for its mysteries, and Ilion, where as a cultivated woman she wanted to commune with her soul. She even had an accident while crossing the Scamander river not far from Ilion, when the water suddenly rose; she was traveling incognito in a litter, but Agrippa was angry that the inhabitants had not brought any assistance to his wife, and he imposed a fine on them.

One of the most thorough journeys was made by the elder Agrippina when she accompanied Germanicus. The conditions were ideal, since Germanicus was armed with powers everywhere superior to those of the governors of the transoceanic provinces. His mission was a kind of inspection tour, but without an express purpose, unless it was to set everything in order on his way. Time was no object.

The couple was away for a long time, leaving several children in Rome and taking others with them, surrounded by a large group of friends outstanding in war and in letters. A veritable flotilla sailed with the autumn current from Ancona, the Adriatic port. The first visit was a brotherly one, to see Drusus in Dalmatia on the other side of the Adriatic. But although the two brothers got on admirably, the sisters-in-law were jealous of each other.

Then after following along the picturesque Dalmatian coast, with its islands drawn up parallel to the shore, they reached the Ionian Sea. But because of a slightly delayed departure the sea was constantly rough; and in January a halt of several days was necessary for repairing the ships at Nicopolis in Epirus. This lapse of time allowed the passengers to make a land excursion of about twelve-and-a-half miles to see the bays made famous by the Battle of Actium. It was a familial pilgrimage, since each visitor had ancestors among those who fought on that day. Augustus and Mark Antony, the two adversaries in this battle which determined their fate, were respectively the great-uncle and grandfather of Germanicus, and the grandfather and great-uncle of Agrippina! Almost all the great names in Rome had been on one side or the other. The trophies raised to Augustus the conqueror, and the camp of the vanquished Antony were images both of glory and of sorrow.

Next came the traditional visit to one of the queens of the ancient world – Athens, the supremely beautiful city. Her un-damaged monuments and her intellectual activity made her the uncontested center of Greece in the imperial epoch. Although out of respect for the ancient city Germanicus entered it with only one lictor and no other display, the Athenians received him and his family with the most flattering honors, and statues were dedicated to them.

From Athens they crossed the Euripos, a narrow arm of the sea which separates the mainland from the island of Euboea, and then after a longer sail on the Aegean Sea the fleet reached Lesbos, off Ionia. They were in Asia, very far from Rome, on an island where it was pleasant to stay. Many Romans had already come to live there, among them Julia, who had probably given birth there to Agrippina. The latter was honored as a native of the place; she was honored with the title of Aeolian goddess. Their stay was to be much longer still, for Agrippina gave birth there to her last child, Julia.

EUXINE SEA [BLACK SEA]
Sinope
PAPHLAGONIA
Nicomedia
BITHYNIA
PONTUS
Halys
Caesarea
Laodicea
CAPPADOCIA
Commagene
ARMENIA
Artaxata
Tigris
Tralles
PAMPHYLIA
Cyrrhestice
Antioch
LYCIA
Attalia
Patara
CYPRUS
euphrates
SYRIA
Jordan
PALESTINE
Dead Sea
N
ARABIA
PETRAEA
Petra
PT
RED SEA
Nile
TO Elephantine
Coptos

After a long rest on Lesbos, the couple set off again. But their itinerary became less ordinary, more detailed than that of a normal official or a tourist. Germanicus' rank, the time at his disposal, and his natural curiosity got them involved. Abandoning the coast of Asia Minor for a while, the flotilla sailed to Perinth and Byzantium, city of the Dardanelles, and then probably entered the Euxine Sea (The Black Sea). These places, colonized by the Greeks in the eighth century B.C. and then more or less annexed and protected by the Romans, were the far out-of-the-way corners of the empire.

On the way back, the contrary north wind prevented a landing at Samothrace, where our travelers would have liked to attend the celebrated mysteries. The route along the coasts of Asia Minor became more standard: Ilium, Colophon, where the oracle of Apollo of Claros was consulted, Ephesus, and Rhodes, one of the most active commercial centers of the Mediterranean. A series of trips inland took the travelers to Pergamum, city of terraces, and then, far in the center of the Armenian kingdom between the Black Sea and the Caspian Sea, Germanicus went to crown a king.

Finally they landed on the shores of one of the empire's most turbulent provinces: Syria. At Antioch, conflicts arose with the new governor of the province, Piso, and his wife Plancina. These two did not miss an opportunity to criticize Agrippina and Germanicus, even in public. The orders that were given were badly executed, and the local tribes became restive. Sick of all these quarrels, Germanicus escaped to Egypt. He got rid of his military escort and parted with certain associates. He walked with bare feet, dressed completely in the Greek fashion. For a Roman, this was a sign of total relaxation. Egypt at that time was a world apart. Alexandria was famous for its excitement and activity; the Pharos, the museum, the library, Alexander's tomb constituted so many intellectual allurements; the port and the warehouses made it one of the cities on which the grain supply of Rome depended. Beyond Alexandria and the pleasure city of Canopus, the world of ancient Egypt began: Thebes, and still farther away, Syene, and Elephantine. At the first cataract one was at the edge of the Roman world, facing the unknown.

On returning to Antioch, Germanicus fell ill and died in a frightful atmosphere of hatred and suspicion, believing that he had been poisoned by Piso. Agrippina, ill and broken with grief, embarked as quickly as possible with her children and her hus-

Syria (Palmyra).

band's ashes. Winter weather did not prevent this mournful return. At Brundusium, in the midst of a huge crowd turned out to welcome her, the young widow of thirty-three appeared, flanked by two of her children and carrying in her arms the funerary urn. Happily, all journeys did not have such dramatic homecomings.

For cultured women, travel did not only have the charms of

The apotheosis of Germanicus.

tourism. While in Rome, particularly at the beginning of the empire, custom forbade them any show of power, they enjoyed greater liberty in the provinces. On the one hand, the inhabitants did not hesitate to confer unusual honors on men and women; and on the other hand, what opportunities for political activity! Outside Rome the sense of freedom of action was so much more real that save for rare exceptions the court rivalries were forgotten. This explains Caecina Severus and his diatribe against

magistrates' wives who followed their husbands into the provinces. We can understand it still better if we look at the list of honors conferred on women and study feminine political activity outside Rome.

In antiquity it was rather a common thing to give honors to a visitor, and these honors were minutely codified, organized around many 'themes.' When a celebrated traveler paid a visit to a city, it was customary to erect a statue to him or dedicate a monument; sometimes he was also raised to the dignity of honorary citizen. These distinctions were offered to famous artists, actors, singers, and sculptors, or to professors – all the nomadic professions. With greater reason, travelers representing authority were also the object of honors, but where they were concerned the custom was subject to change.

Modern nations sometimes issue a series of postage stamps in commemoration of an event; in those days, coins were struck. A certain number of Greek cities had kept the privilege of coining money. Portraits of the members of the imperial family who had traveled in the East were thus modeled in profile on coins from the various cities they had visited. In addition to the portrait, there would be the representation of an event or a symbol of the person's life. And so on Lesbos, Julia was shown in the likeness of Mother Venus, and her daughter Agrippina as Ceres bearing fruit. The notion of fecundity that was associated with them recalled their confinements; but for Julia the blood of Caesar was added, or the notion of beauty, while Agrippina's chief attribute remained the number of her children. Livia was represented as piety, as justice, or perhaps as the goddess of health or as Juno.

This phenomenon of deification continued to grow during the course of the empire. For a while the deification of emperors and members of their family was an Oriental novelty, shocking to the Roman spirit which still recoiled from the title of king. The foresight of Augustus and Tiberius caused them to refuse all deification in Rome, although after the Emperor's death Livia was to organize the cult of the Divine Augustus all over the empire. Meanwhile, despite all these refusals based on clever policy, the living emperor ended up being worshiped as a god, and this cult addressed to his image was to serve as a spiritual bond among all the religions except the Jews and, soon after, the Christians. In any case, in the Oriental provinces people anticipated the authorizations. For centuries the Asiatic peoples had likened the sovereign to a god, and this 'barbaric' notion ended by taking root, although it met with a certain irony in Greek countries after the dismemberment of Alexander's empire. For the Oriental populations it was nothing less than a matter of prestige. And so Augustus and Tiberius themselves shut their eyes; they refrained from forbidding a custom which was useful to them.

To be a lady of rank and see oneself promoted to the level of goddess! And it was all the easier to enter into the 'spirit of the character,' since speeches of welcome and of tribute serenely insisted and embroidered indefinitely on the theme of divinity. These Oriental peoples knew how to honor their guests in a way to turn the heads of Romans themselves: what about the heavy golden crowns offered to Agrippina and Germanicus in the course of a feast given by the king of the Nabathians? Was not Julius Caesar assassinated less than sixty years before because he had dared make a show of wearing a crown on his head?

How can it be surprising that after such honors, 'forgetting what is suitable to their sex' – as 'old Romans' put it – women took part in politics? Unfortunately, to engage in political activity, if one was a woman and consequently did not occupy public office, was too often to be content with its rather murky side issues. The accusation most often leveled against governor's wives was that of greed. According to the sharp-tongued Martial and Juvenal, the lady was tempted to profit by her husband's position 'to fleece the provincials.' It is certain that Plancina allowed herself to be bribed by a dethroned king of Armenia who was negotiating with her husband. A severe law was passed in Tiberius' reign, aimed at counteracting misappropriation of funds and at combating the reasons for criticizing the wives of officials. Every magistrate was made responsible for wrongs incurred by provincials in dealing with his wife, whether he himself was innocent or ignorant of her machinations and malpractice.

In contrast to these critics, Seneca speaks of his aunt Helvia, and sketches the portrait of 'the ideal governor's wife.' This lady was in fact endowed with a quantity of unusual virtues. She accompanied her husband, the prefect of Egypt, into the most mocking city in the world, the temptress Alexandria. This land of Egypt, so gossipy, so quick and ingenious in disparaging its prefects, where the most irreproachable were not shielded from calumny, this country which carried a taste for joking so far as to despise danger, completely repressed its intemperate tongue and admired Helvia as an incomparable model of virtue. And what was the formula for such magnificent success, of which Seneca tells us, not without exaggeration: 'It would mean much to have been applauded by her province during all sixteen years; it is still more glorious to have remained ignored by it . . . '? Here it is; it is characteristic: Helvia never appeared in public, she never received any inhabitant of the province in her house, never asked anything of her husband, never allowed herself to be solicited . . . .

But to get back to another reality. If it was quite serious to try to get rich by shady methods, to accept sumptuous gifts from sovereigns coming to negotiate, it was inadmissible to show off, not only at feasts, but before the troops.

Ancient historians have described some of the military interventions of Roman ladies at the beginning of the empire. For the Romans, it was an intolerable interference on the part of women in a domain that did not concern them. The Roman military tradition was purely masculine: there were heroes, but no warrior heroines. It was all right for barbarians, Germans or Britons, to fight under a queen's orders or with the aid of 'female hordes' who with cries of hatred and pain prevented the men from surrendering, or even, if the battle were lost, killed their own babies before strangling themselves with their own hands. For a long time Roman civilization had been past the stage where war represented a vital necessity for the entire population. It was not the time for women to get interested in the army. And so it is with indignation that Tacitus tells how Plancina, wife of the Syrian governor, reviewed the troops.

The role taken by Agrippina the Elder in the armies of Germania was to appear much more important and even still more serious. Her conduct lent itself to serious criticism on the part of Tiberius, who was always suspicious; everything leads one to believe that the fierce diatribe of Caecina Severus was indirectly aimed at this princess. Since Tiberius was not fond of her, it was a good way of courting this emperor, who was, after all, a misogynist.

To get on to the facts: at first Agrippina never left her husband, even when she was pregnant or when the frontier was unsafe. In spite of the dark reputation of the German forests, she bore children in these remote places. Among those born at that time, a daughter survived to whom history was to pay much attention: the Empress Agrippina. Later she was to found a colony in the place where she was born, which was given her name. She christened it Colonia Agrippina – it became the modern Cologne. At least one other child accompanied Agrippina the Elder with the army, and the soldiers doted on this little boy raised in camp. They named him the 'foster-child of the legions,' or 'caligula,' which may be translated 'little boot.' Was it not his mother's idea to have him wear miniature army boots?

It is wrong, however, to imagine this lady camping in a tent. Access to a Roman camp was legally forbidden to women. But around the stationary camp where the legions were quartered along the frontier were houses built and inhabited by canteen keepers, suppliers, and various shop keepers. Agrippina, Germanicus, and their numerous train probably lived there.

Their presence produced rather unusual results. In 14 A.D. after Augustus' death, the legions under Germanicus rebelled; they claimed the bounty Augustus would have bequeathed them, and showed themselves ready to hail Germanicus as emperor. Germanicus' sincere, stirring speeches and donations of money did not succeed in calming the soldiers, whose lack of control increased. The arrival of senators sent by Tiberius aggravated the situation still further.

In the bewilderment of terror and conscious guilt they were penetrated by an apprehension that persons had come at the Senate's orders to cancel the concessions they had extorted by mutiny . . . . At midnight they began to demand the Imperial standard kept in Germanicus' quarters, and having rushed together to the entrance, burst the door, dragged Caesar from his bed, and forced him by threats of death to give up the standard. Then roaming through the camp-streets, they met the envoys, who on hearing of the tumult were hastening to Germanicus. They loaded them with insults, and were on the point of murdering them, Plancus especially, whose high rank had deterred him from flight. In his peril he found safety only in the camp of the first legion. There clasping the standards and eagle, he sought to protect himself under their sanctity. And had not the eagle-bearer, Calpurnius, saved him from the worst violence, the blood of an envoy of the Roman people would in a Roman camp have stained the altars of the gods, an occurrence rare even among our foes . . . . At last with the light of day, when the general and the soldiers and whole affair were clearly recognized, Germanicus entered the camp . . . .

He made another speech, stunned his hearers rather than calming them, and dismissed the envoys.

In the midst of this tumult, Germanicus' friends, disturbed, reproached him for his indecision and advised him at least to send away his pregnant wife and little son. Germanicus hesitated a long time.

When his wife spurned the notion, protesting that she was a descendant of the Divine Augustus and could face peril with no degenerate spirit, he at last embraced her and the son of their love with many tears, and after long delay compelled them to depart. Slowly, a pitiable procession of women moved along, a general's fugitive wife with a little son in her bossom, her friends' wives weeping round her, as with her they were dragging themselves from the camp. Not less sorrowful were these who remained . . . . There was no appearance of the triumphant general about Germanicus, and he seemed to be in a conquered city rather than in his own camp, while groans and wailings attracted the ears and looks even of the soldiers. They came out of their tents, asking 'What was that mournful sound? What meant the sad sight? Here were ladies of rank, not a centurion to escort them, not a soldier, no sign of a prince's wife, none of the usual retinue. Could they be going to the Treveri, to be subjects of the foreigner?' Then they felt shame and pity, and remembered her father Agrippa, her grandfather Augustus, her father-in-law Drusus, her own glory as a mother of children, her noble purity. And there was her little child too, born in the camp, brought up amid the tents of the legions . . . . But nothing moved them so much as jealousy towards the Treveri. They entreated, stopped the way, that Agrippina might return and remain, some running to meet her, while most of them went back to Germanicus. He, with grief and anger that were yet fresh . . . began to address the throng around him . . . . Thereupon, as suppliants confessing that his reproaches were true, they implored him to . . . recall his wife, to let the nursling of the legions return . . . .

After this last incident the revolt calmed down. Germanicus took his soldiers on a long excursion into enemy territory.

So it was that the appearance of Agrippina and her son on the point of departure transformed the madmen into suppliants. It was an indication of the soldiers' jealousy of the Treveri.

certainly, but also proof of the personal popularity of the 'General's lady.' Tiberius was to conclude from it that in the eyes of the army Agrippina's power was superior to that of the officers: a woman had stifled an uprising against which the name of the prince had been powerless. Now, Agrippina's personal action does seems of a limited kind; but what about that which she initiated?

That happened in 15 A.D. Germanicus as usual had prepared his summer campaign, but wishing to create a surprise, he took the offensive at the beginning of spring and suddenly fell upon a neighboring people, the Chatti. He chose four legions, five thousand auxiliary troops hastily raised among the Germans on this side of the Rhine, and entrusted them to Caecina; he himself took as many with him. The first invasion against the Chatti was followed by success. But one of the German leaders, Arminius, whose pregnant wife was a Roman prisoner, roused a whole series of bordering nations against the Romans. Germanicus sent Caecina toward the Ems, and he himself penetrated into the interior. There he found traces of one of the legions of Varus, the Roman general who had let himself be led astray with his troops into a forest from which none came out alive. Germanicus pushed on to the forest of Teuteburg, in which, it is said, lay the unburied remains of Varus and his legions. He buried them – a fitting end to a disaster which had provoked the tears and despair of Augustus.

Setting out in pursuit of Arminius, who was trying to reach impenetrable places, Germanicus plunged deep into woods and little-known marshes, where the Romans were soon in a sorry situation. Caecina, for his part, was isolated on the Ems at Long Bridges. Panic seized the Romans, who thought of Varus' fate, while the Germans felt sure of themselves and of victory.

In the rear, all news was awaited with anxiety. There was rejoicing over successes, but suddenly 'the rumor spread that the army had been surprised and that the Germans were marching threateningly on the Gauls.' On the heels of this rumor came panic. With the cowardice characteristic of people who have been well protected and make fun of war because they have not suffered from it, and panic-stricken that the barbarians might come and massacre them, the Gauls wanted to destroy the bridge across the Rhine. The Germans could only get across by boat and so they would be stopped. But the Roman legions then would also be imprisoned, as it were, on the other side of the

Rhine. A woman opposed this 'infamy' – to save her husband, doubtless, but also to save the legions and the honor of Rome: it was Agrippina. She at that time made use of all the authority she might possess and during those days assumed the role of a leader. In fact, she actually replaced her absent husband. She remained at the head of the bridge and directed the defense. Having brought the reactions of the rear under control, she

Parthian and German captives

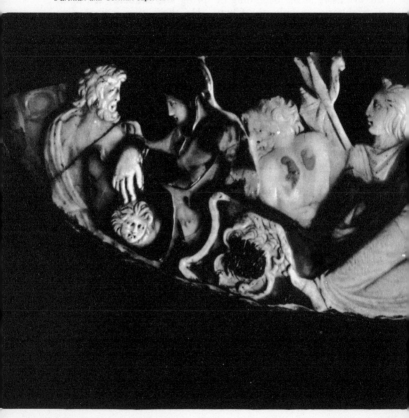

mustered the troops. Standing at the bridgehead, she addressed
the retreating legions with praise and thanks. Each returned to
his camp in order. She distributed dressings and clothing. When
Germanicus returned, it was to soldiers that he could speak and
not a routed rabble.

Here a woman indeed had reviewed the troops and 'taken
liberties.' What did they make of that in Rome?

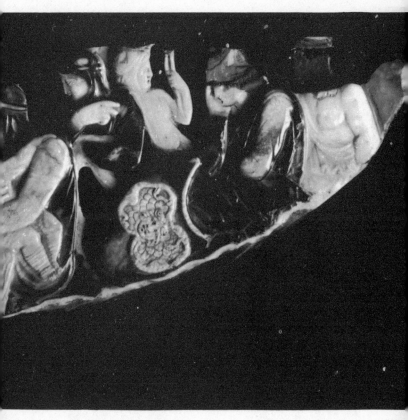

Politics

In Rome the political role of women follows a curve parallel to the creation, consolidation, and total power of that new form of authority, the principate.

Under the republic many women 'went into politics' without having direct access to it; witness one of Caesar's mistresses, Servilia, the mother of Brutus. Women had taken part in the Catiline conspiracy. Of one of them, Sempronia, Sallust has left us a famous savage portrait, very characteristic of the conceptions of the period:

> Now among these women was Sempronia, who had often committed many crimes of masculine daring. In birth and beauty, in her husband also and children, she was abundantly favoured by fortune; well read in the literature of Greece and Rome, able to play the lyre and dance more skillfully than an honest woman need, and having many other accomplishments which minister to voluptuousness. But there was nothing which she held so cheap as modesty and chastity; you could not easily say whether she was less sparing of her money or her honor; her desires were so ardent that she sought men more often then she was sought by them. Even before the time of the conspiracy she had often broken her word, repudiated her debts, been privy to murder; poverty and extravangance combined had driven her headlong. Nevertheless, she was a woman of no mean endowments; she could write verses, bandy jests, and use language which was modest, or tender, or wanton; in fine, she possessed a high degree of wit and of charm.

Besides this Sempronia – whom we do not know in other connections – we have already met Fulvia, Antony's wife, raising troops and leading the Perugian war. This was not her first attempt, and her political activity would merit special study: it was she who revealed to Cicero the secrets of the Catiline conspiracy.

Then, there could be no question of titles and special honors. By definition, action on the part of women was a source of scandal, and shameful reasons or purposes were always attributed to them. Sallust emphasizes Sempronia's taste for luxury and debauchery. As for Fulvia, Martial quotes six lewd lines of Augustus' which would confer a simple motive of passion on her warlike enterprise . . . . Political propaganda doubtless has these necessities! It is nonetheless true that the influence of women in political matters was quite comparable to that of their remote descendants in the Third Republic.

The program of moral order which the principate wished to establish was distrustful of women. Octavius suffered from particular resentment. Fulvia had held him in check for a year; and there had been that supreme *femme fatale*, Cleopatra. This famous Egyptian queen, who caused the flow of so much blood and so much ink, had been the focus of a goodly amount of hatred, disdain, and admiration as well. Ten years after Actium, the loves of Antony and Cleopatra were a constantly utilized poetic subject – that of a love which is fatal to the man. Augustus' contemporaries traced a portrait of deliberate malice in Cleopatra. Of course, Octavius had much to fear from a woman who had borne a son to Caesar; and this foreign queen, whom Caesar brought back to Rome not to adorn his triumph but to install sumptuously in a house across the Tiber, had caused a scandal. It seems probable that Cleopatra's presence added to the reasons which determined the dictator's assassination. When Antony in his turn fell in love with the queen and passionately, too, it seems, Octavius had everything to fear. Did Antony recognize little Caesarion as Caesar's son? Did not the ambitious Egyptian queen intend to regroup around her nation all the little kingdoms protected by Rome in the East? And Antony seemed to share this conception of Eastern policy.

And so Octavius, and then Augustus, would tend to present Antony as a man softened by love, magically enthralled by a Cleopatra who was half a sorceress and an accomplished courtesan, a Cleopatra who dreamed of ruling the world and was sunk in debauchery. Propertius, Horace, Ovid – each one in turn blackened the picture on a moral and political level. Here is a passage that gives the tone:

> . . . Jove brings shame on himself and on his house. Why should I tell of her that of late heaped insults on our arms, that woman who found lovers even among her slaves, and claimed the walls of Rome and the Senate enslaved to her tyranny as a fee from her foul paramour? Guilty Alexandria, land most skilled in guile, and Memphis so often bloodstained with our woe, where the sand robbed Pompey of his three triumphs! No day shall ever free thee of this stain, O Rome! Better for thee, Pompey, had thy funeral gone forth on the Phlegrean plain, or hadst thou been doomed to bow thy neck to thy wife's father! Forsooth the harlot queen of unchaste Canopus, the one disgrace branded on Rome by the race of Philip, dared to match barking Anubis against our Roman Jove, to force Tiber to endure the threats of Nile, to drive out the Roman trumpet with rattling sistrum and in the poled barge pursue the Liburnian galley, to stretch her foul curtains on the Tarpeian rock, and to give judgment amid the arms and statues of Marius. . . .Yet didst thou fly, O queen, to the wandering streams of timorous Nile! Thy hands received the chains of Rome. I saw her limbs bitten by the sacred asps, I saw her limbs drink in slumber as it worked its secret way. . . .

Propertius cannot be blamed for letting go about her love affairs, when 'the city high-throned on the seven hills, the queen of all the world, was terrified by a woman's might and feared her threats!'

The attitude toward women adopted by the regime took exception to this desire for power attributed to Cleopatra. A work of Propertius, called 'the queen of the elegies,' expresses it quite well: a young woman, daughter of Scribonia, prepares to die. She draws up a balance sheet of her life. This Cornelia, a historical and not imaginary character, appears somewhat like the ideal Roman woman of the time, when she exclaims that 'the supreme triumph of a woman is her good reputation!' This reputation – which was freely elaborated on around her funerary monument – was composed of two elements, also traditional in all Augustan literature: chastity, which really seems a rare thing since so much was made of it; and fecundity, the certificate of a good Roman citizeness. The supreme triumph of which Cornelia speaks must even be understood in the Roman military sense of the term. But we must not be deceived. Although it became the standard and right-thinking thing to hold up the chastity and fecundity of the matron in opposition to the Oriental debauchery of Cleopatra, the latter enjoyed an unquestionable prestige among the great ladies of the period. And the poets, official as they might be, could not prevent their admiration from showing through occasionally:

When she took flight, Caesar increased the strength of his oars to sweep down upon her like a sparrow-hawk upon a timid dove . . . He desired to capture the fatal monster. But she, jealous of a better death, did not show a woman's fear before the sword. She took no advantage of her swift ships to seek shelter in a hidden land. She dared to gaze with a serene countenance on the ruins of her power, to handle without fear the snakes with their murderous fangs, that she might fill her body with their poison. This voluntary death glorifies her – proud woman, she refused our sinister ships the honor of bearing her ruined majesty in glorious triumph.

And so it was good form to be shocked by Cleopatra – but she was imitated in private, whether for her amorous successes or in her political activities. Messalina, the younger Agrippina, and Poppaea among others were Cleopatras in a small way, replicas more or less accurate or accentuated. But to get to that point took time. In Rome itself, honors and official authority were to come by slow and difficult conquest, and power once achieved, though often considerable, was always to be precarious.

To take cognizance of the female political role is to make a distinction between official privileges and hidden power. The latter we are sure was sometimes very great, but to gather concrete proofs of it is something else, as one may easily understand. Augustus' wife Livia certainly played an important role during her husband's lifetime. However, the texts inform us that she was never seen outside her home except at religious ceremonies. But what about her husband's habit of first writing down what he meant to say to her? It was certainly not in order to speak to her about the care of his togas or the quality of the cooking!

There are abundant famous examples of Livia's hidden influence. The best known is the one Seneca chooses in *De Cle-*

134

mentia, and of which Dio Cassius also gives a significant account. A conspiracy had just been discovered against Augustus on the part of Cinna:

Augustus did not know what decision to make, and could not pass the day without worrying or the night without alarm. Livia finally said to him, 'What is the matter, my husband? why do you not sleep?' Augustus told his story in the darkness, and explained in detail all his fears and doubts. Livia first answered him, 'You are right, but I have a piece of advice to give you, if you will accept it and if you do not think it wicked for a woman to give an opinion which no one among your best friends would dare mention, not for lack of knowledge of the matter but for lack of boldness in speaking of it.' After this preamble, and since Augustus could only beg her to continue, she added, 'I will speak without fear, as one who shares your joys and sorrows, who reigns with you in your health and strength and who, should anything befall you (may it never occur), will perish with you.'

And Livia urged Augustus to a gesture of clemency which won for the Prince the affection of the citizens to the extent – we are told – that there were actually no further conspiracies.

Under Tiberius, the most misogynistic of the emperors – and with reason – it was still a woman who most discreetly saved the Prince from a singularly grave danger. Sejanus' influence was growing day by day, and the boldness of this knight, the Emperor's favorite, knew no bounds. In 31 A.D. all family obstacles had been removed; Tiberius' son Drusus was dead, the remainder of Germanicus' offspring were not in a position to intervene; and Sejanus was consul with Tiberius. He enjoyed the imperial confidence and ruled the senate. We know he organized a vast conspiracy to get rid of Tiberius. Who was to prevent him? The Emperor lived in isolation on Capri, and his contacts with the rest of the world were essentially made through Sejanus. It was then that Antonia, the Emperor's sister-in-law, who remained in Rome, got wind of the intrigue. She described everything in detail in a letter which she entrusted to her most loyal slave, and despatched him to Capri. This implies a network of contacts that was far-reaching, to say the least, for a lady living in retirement. Besides, the only two women in whom Tiberius had confidence were his first wife, Vipsania Agrippina, and

Antonia, his sister-in-law. After this signal service, the latter really had Tiberius' ear, and we see her interceding for one of her friends, Agrippa, the young king of the Jews, who had some serious trouble with the Emperor.

Later we can also predict the influence of a Messalina or a Poppaea, through more official privileges. We see them assisting their husbands at palace receptions, and especially on the occasion of lawsuits brought up before the emperor. When Messalina decided on the ruin of Valerius Asiaticus, whose magnificent gardens she coveted, she was present in Claudius' room when the accused appeared before the Emperor. He caused her to shed tears, but as soon as Valerius Asiaticus had convinced and softened everyone, especially Claudius, Messalina left the room to dry her tears and to warn her friend Vitellius not to allow the accused to escape . . . .

These few examples, taken from many others and chosen

Nero and Poppaea in "Quo Vadis?"

intentionally for not being concerned with these ladies' essential preoccupation, the succession to the empire, demonstrate the somewhat obvious political influence of women. But this activity had to remain discreet to be effective, since the awarding of official honors was scandalous. Even those who achieved a power of which everyone was aware were constrained to adopt a certain reserve. The most typical case is that of the all-powerful Empress Agrippina. When through her Nero was made emperor, it was unquestionably she who governed in his place. Everyone knew it – and was also quite shocked. What did she miss? Taking part in the sessions of the senate. Never mind: as was done in the days of Augustus' old age, the senate convened at the palace, and Agrippina was present at the session. But it was necessary to respect custom and propriety: no one saw her. She entered by a concealed door after the senators and remained hidden by a curtain. She heard without being seen; and consequently she was unable to intervene directly. And so the result was that despite all her authority she could not prevent the young Nero from giving back to the senate a series of prerogatives that Claudius had withdrawn from it. With the Empress Agrippina the paradox came to its climax: the more a woman enjoyed official privileges, the more her actual power was contested and insecure.

Livia died in her bed at the age of eighty-six, after a long life of often difficult and hard-won achievements, at odds with her son Tiberius, whom she had placed under too much obligation. But Tiberius, who would not take the trouble to see his sick mother again nor come to the funeral, and whose resentment burst out constantly, went away from Rome, disappeared. The aged Livia, envied but honored, preserved her influence.

Agrippina died at forty-five, assassinated with unusual premeditation by order of her son, having known loneliness and the progressive decline of her power. And everyone seems to have been so much in league against her that in spite of the enormity of the crime, no one missed her.

From the one to the other of these two women who dominated the beginning and the end of the entire epoch a whole evolution took place, which corresponds to that of the imperial power. The fact that Agrippina came to a violent end despite her great power is consistent with this evolution, since Caligula, Claudius, and Nero – her brother, husband, and son – were also murdered, while Augustus died in honored old age, and Tiberius, though hated, lived out his natural term.

The official honors accorded to women trailed those of men, and this usually by the express wish of the emperors. During Augustus' lifetime, however, important privileges were granted to the two most outstanding women in his family, even before the Prince's power had reached its peak, at the time of the triumvirate. The beneficiaries were Octavia and Livia. They obtained their emancipation first – and many Roman women thereafter sought to benefit by a like privilege. This was a cardinal innovation: Octavia and Livia achieved the power, in the year 35 B.C. of freely and personally administering their property without being responsible to a guardian. The free management of her possessions – this right only exists for the unmarried in modern French civilization, where women nevertheless vote and have access to a political career and to the government. In the Roman period, where scarcely any point was made of 'feminism' and the woman always submitted to the control of a guardian: father, husband, or a guardian of her own choice (in this case almost never the husband), this innovation was full of consequences. It confirmed, at all events, the importance and activity of Roman ladies as 'women of affairs.' Some of them amassed immense fortunes. This is notable in the case of Antonia, who inherited considerable property in Asia from her father Antony, which she administered and increased with great success. Women often became financial powers: Antonia thus lent huge sums of money to Agrippa, the young king of the Jews, whom she liked very much. The moral consequences of this financial independence were also important – it facilitated divorce.

But to return to the honors accorded to Livia and Octavia in 35 B.C. They were permitted to have statues made of them, which truly placed them on the level of official personages. Finally, an outstanding privilege, they were declared 'sacrosanct,' which meant they were inviolable, like the tribunes of the people. To commit a crime against them was an offense against religion.

Much later, after the death of Drusus, Livia also acquired as an exceptional favor the distinction granted to mothers of three children, although she only had two. That was because the sterility of her second marriage seemed irremediable and not deliberate.

In her position as Augustus' wife during the Emperor's lifetime, Livia's official role seems to have been much restricted: she dedicated a temple with Tiberius, at one of the latter's triumphs, and a portico at Posilipo bears her name. Octavia also had a portico built which became a public walk highly prized by the Romans. We have already seen Livia, accompanied by Julia, giving a banquet for the women of Rome, after Tiberius' victories, while their husbands were giving one for the men. But this called for nothing in contrast to republican customs.

When Augustus died, he did not forget his wife in his will. The most important legacy was undoubtedly the decision, put off until then, to adopt Livia into the familiy and thus to confer upon her the name of Julia Augusta. 'Augusta' established the sacred title of the empress; from then on it was to be the supreme surname sought by all women of the imperial family.

All this had been granted by Augustus; and then it was the senate's turn to chime in and propose honors for women, just at the time of Tiberius' accession. Whenever that illustrious assembly spoke, it was to multiply acts of adulation toward Augustus and his wife. It was suggested that the title of 'Mother' be conferred on Livia, or of 'Mother of the Country,' or even (a less tactful suggestion) that Tiberius be given the name of 'Son of Augusta' – the unfortunate Tiberius, who already felt on his shoulders the weight of that relationship! His indignation knew no bounds, and he rejected all honors proposed for his mother. He even refused to have her accompanied by a lictor. He never ceased repeating that it was necessary to reduce the honors granted to women. The truth, states Tacitus, was that jealousy tormented him, and he felt the elevation of a women as a belittling of himself. It was only too true that he owed his position to his capacity as 'Livia's son'! During his entire reign Tiberius carefully avoided placing his mother in the limelight, since her actual power annoyed him. In 23 A.D., he forbade her the imperial box at the theater; she sat among the vestals, to 'honor them with her presence,' and in order to increase the prestige of the priests and arouse their religious zeal.

When Livia died, the funeral was modest. Tiberius opposed the post mortem honors which the senate wished to bestow, particularly the apotheosis which would have transformed his mother into a goddess, on a level with Caesar and Augustus. It was not until the reign of Claudius, the grandson whom she had often called an imbecile, that divine honors were granted to Livia, the apotheosis refused by her son. She then took her place, like Augustus, in the procession which filed out before the performance at the circus and presented the whole imperial family, living or dead, in effigy or in reality, on chariots drawn by elephants.

It must be remarked that honors were always more easily bestowed post mortem than during the lifetime of the persons in question, and this was true for both men and women. It even seems that people were most honored at their funerals. A funeral elegy for the deceased was always read. An annual sacrifice might be offered in his memory, on his birthday or on certain important dates in his life. The College of Priests or occasionally the vestals were in charge of this ceremony; it was basically a religious act. The manner in which the image of the deceased appeared in the procession before the circus was also significant; the way in which it was carried, the style of chariot which bore it, the species of animal drawing the chariot, all had meaning. Claudius and Caligula each offered chariots to their mothers, Antonia and the elder Agrippina. In some cases, finally, deification was achieved. Claudius decreed the apotheosis of Livia; some years before, a sister of Caligula had already been treated as a goddess – Drusilla, with whom the Emperor had fallen in love, to the point not only of incestuous relations but even of making her heiress to his fortune and to the empire. Drusilla died first; and Caligula ordered a complete suspension of affairs. It was a capital crime to laugh, to go to the baths, to have dinner with parents, wife, and children. She was deified, and in all circumstances, even the most solemn, in assembly and before the people or the soldiers, Caligula thereafter swore only by the divinity of Drusilla. In the same way, when his wife Poppaea Sabina died, Nero had a temple built at the expense of the Roman matrons in honor of 'Venus Sabina.' A daughter of Nero and this same Poppaea, dead at the age of four months, had also been deified!

With Caligula and Nero we are at the end of the evolution; they were both half-mad. Caligula set up an actual Egyptian monarchy and considered himself a god on earth: he thus had to marry his sister. As for Nero, he thought everything permissible to him and acted accordingly.

Posthumous honors, however lofty, are nevertheless not so pleasant as those which can be enjoyed during life. And so most women sought the outward and visible signs of power as forcibly and decorously as the Roman temperament permitted. Livia scarcely went out; she only attended religious functions. Soon, to figure in official ceremonies and (what is more) to be there in an important capacity, where the women of imperial blood could feel themselves equal to the master, became the most common ambition. What could be more masculine than a triumph, a military ceremony celebrated after a great victory, when before all Rome the heaped-up booty and chained captives marched by behind the victor's chariot? When Claudius triumphed over the Britons, a litter followed the Emperor's richly decorated chariot; Messalina also 'triumphed'! She loved all the things of this world, and her interference in political matters consisted of nothing but expropriations and vengeance, as her fancy willed. When the women had more ambition, their power, even officially, was very different. The younger Agrippina, Claudius' last wife, seems to have been the ambitious type. Her whole life was concentrated on an uninterrupted course toward power, both official and unofficial. A revealing sentence can be found in the work of Tacitus, who did not like her and disapproved of the part she played. As soon as Agrippina was married to Claudius,

> . . . there came a revolution in the State, and everything was under the control of a woman, who did not, like Messalina, insult Rome by loose manners. It was a stringent, and, so to say, masculine despotism; there was sternness and generally arrogance in public, no sort of immodesty at home, unless it conduced to power. A boundless greed of wealth was veiled under the pretext that riches were being accumulated as a prop to the throne.

Certainly Agrippina displayed sternness and arrogance in public, but, unlike Livia, she did appear in public; she presided beside her husband, dressed in sumptuous clothing and seated on a chair that was like a throne.

The Britons were the cause of one of the most startling manifestations of these privileges. One of their leaders, Caractacus, in a battle against the Romans, had taken over the leadership of a whole group of British tribes. At the outcome of the battle, the wife, daughter, and brothers of this leader were taken prisoner.

> There is seldom safety for the unfortunate, and Caractacus, seeking the protection of Cartismandua, queen of the Brigantes, was put in chains and delivered up to the conquerors, nine years after the beginning of the war in Britain. His fame had

spread thence, and traveled to the neighbouring islands and provinces, and was actually celebrated in Italy. All were eager to see the great man, who for so many years had defied our power. Even at Rome, the name of Caractacus was no obscure one; and the Emperor, while he exalted his own glory, enhanced the renown of the vanquished. The people were summoned as to a grand spectacle; the praetorian cohort were drawn up under arms in the plain in front of their camp; then came a procession of the royal vassals, and the ornaments and neck-chains and the spoils which the king had won in wars with other tribes, were displayed. Next were to be seen his brothers, his wife and daughter; last of all, Caractacus himself. All the rest stooped in their too abject supplication; not so the king, who neither by humble look nor speech sought compassion . . . . When he was set before the Emperor's tribunal, he spoke as follows: 'Had my moderation in prosperity been equal to my noble birth and fortune, I should have entered this city as your friend rather than as your captive; and you should not have disdained to receive, under a treaty of peace, a king descended from illustrious ancestors and ruling many nations. My present lot is as glorious to you as it is degrading to myself. I had men and horses, arms and wealth. What wonder if I parted with them reluctantly? If you Romans choose to lord it over the world, does it follow that the world is to accept slavery? Were I to have been at once delivered up as a prisoner, neither my fall nor your triumph would have become famous. My punishment would be followed by oblivion, whereas, if you save my life, I shall be an everlasting memorial of your clemency!' Upon this the Emperor granted pardon to Caractacus, to his wife, and to his brothers. Released from their bonds, they did homage also to Agrippina who sat near, conspicuous on another throne, in the same language of praise and gratitude. It was indeed a novelty, quite alien to ancient manners, for a woman to sit in front of Roman standards. In fact, Agrippina boasted that she was herself a partner in the Empire which her ancestors had won.

To this unprecedented honor – sitting before the Roman Army in the sight of all the people like a general at the camp tribunal – Agrippina added others; the title of Augusta, the foundation of a city named for her, 'in order to show her power even before the eyes of the allied peoples,' in the country of the Ubii where she had been born. Finally she entered the capital in a spring chariot, a supreme honor reserved at all times for priests and images of the gods, and which brought to its climax the people's veneration of a woman, daughter of an imperator, sister, wife, and mother of an emperor. She was an extraordinary example.

As the wife of the Emperor, her role is undeniable and her position brilliant. At the death of Claudius, Agrippina installed her son Nero in the place left vacant by the deceased. For some time afterward she saw the honors paid to her increase; she was accompanied by two lictors, like a consul; as Livia had presided over the cult of Augustus, so she presided over that of the deified Claudius. Little by little, however, restrictions to her power appeared. She had to hide behind a curtain to attend the sessions of the senate; and then, a more serious sign, one day when the Armenian ambassadors had come to plead with Nero – and Agrippina proposed to mount the dais and sit beside her son – Nero, under Seneca's influence, forestalled his mother on the pretext of filial piety and prevented the scandal.

Agrippina's power had reached its zenith. From then on it declined. Of course she had succeeded in getting her son on the throne, and we have seen by what means, but a husband is easier to rule than a son. The latter did not hesitate to get rid of her when she became too inconvenient. Titles, honors – the great Roman ladies acquired them as men did, with the establishment of absolute power. Frailty did not exclude authority: their participation in political life proves it.

Women's Part in History

Women had thus sought power like men, and the imperial competition formed the basis of activity for several of them. Masculine rivalries were reflected in parallel battles among the women: the women fought for this or that champion, in such a way that it is possible to view the history of the Julio-Claudian family from the point of view of feminine competition. They deserve to take their place with others in the great book of history. From Livia to the Empress Agrippina, through Agrippina the Elder, the struggles were all the more desperate since, with the vagueness of the qualifications for supreme power and without rules of succession, virtually anything was possible.

The precarious establishment of the empire, with its numerous problems demanding new answers, was Livia's work, in her double role as Augustus' wife and Tiberius' mother. She participated in the installation of the regime and tended to confer on it a moral aspect: always to her own advantage, she rose above intrigues and rivalries. She gives the impression of having achieved what she wanted. Her death during Tiberius' reign made such a gap in political life that it seems possible to speak of a 'reign of Livia': the principate of Tiberius only seems really to begin after the end of this officious reign.

Nothing foreshadowed a brilliant destiny for the daughter of M. Livius Drusus Claudianus, when she was born in January, 58 B.C. Her youth was spent in the midst of the confusion attending the end of the republic. Her family was opposed to Caesar's reign, and her father died in the ranks of Brutus' partisans. She was married to a descendant of one of the oldest

145

patrician families in Rome, the Claudii. In the course of centuries they had always been outstanding for pride and for

LIVIA: *Portrait of Livia as Ceres.*

ambitions which placed them in the foreground, whether in the government or in opposition to it. Livia's first husband, Tiberius Claudius Nero, kept up the tradition: he took up arms – and he was not the only one of his kind – against the young Octavius, Caesar's adopted son who wished to carry on his work. The arrival of this eighteen-year-old on the political scene, this 'child who owed everything to his name,' was unexpected to say the least. And the success of such an adventurer, who disregarded the law with a total lack of scruple, formed a singular complication to the difficult problem of Caesar's succession. After Fulvia and her brother-in-law, L. Antonius, surrendered at the end of the 'Perugian war,' Tiberius Claudius Nero left Italy. We know how Livia, already the mother of Tiberius, fled from Campania and then from Sicily to Sparta, which was under the protection of the Claudian family. She was only eighteen years old.

She returned at a moment of truce between the belligerents. The treaty of Brundusium (40 B.C.) had been concluded between Octavius and Antony, and Octavia, the dearly loved sister of Octavius, had just been married to Antony, the recent widower of the dynamic Fulvia, in token of reconciliation: a truly political union in which Octavia played an important part; she pushed Octavius a little more toward the level of Antony, who appeared in everyone's eyes as the victor and defender – relatively speaking – of tradition. This marriage was celebrated with enthusiasm; all Rome believed in the peace, and Octavia started the fashion of following her husband: both left for Athens where the young wife lived for two years and gave birth to two daughters.

After the reconciliation of Octavius and Antony came reconciliation with Sextus Pompeius. Shortly after the treaty of Brundusium, Octavius married Scribonia, the sister of an important party leader for Sextus Pompeius, the 'King of the Sea,' who held the islands and commanded a huge fleet. This Scribonia had already been twice married to men of consular rank. She had daughters, one of whom, Cornelia, was the subject of a beautiful elegy of Propertius. She was older than Octavius. This marriage was a prelude to the new treaty of Misenum (39 B.C.) which completed the armistice, and a semblance of peace was established among the three principal protagonists. Each, however, held his position; Antony dreamed only of the East; Sextus Pompeius, whose possession of the islands had been acknowledged, held in his hands the provisioning of Rome; Octavius, lord of the West, planned the progressive elimination of the other two. It was at this moment of false total reconciliation that Livia and her husband returned to Rome.

A general overthrow of the alliances then occured. After having presented Octavius with a daughter, Scribonia was cast off on grounds of corrupt morals. Antony, well versed in evil gossip, claimed that she had complained too openly of a courtesan's influence on her husband. Livia's famous marriage occurred immediately thereafter: a mad union of a young wife, six months pregnant, and betrothed, after authorization by the College of Priests, by her first husband. We are told of this thunderbolt of Octavius, said to be so captured by Livia's beauty that he could not wait for her to be delivered .... But this marriage represented a patrician alliance with a great family for Octavius, who was newly raised to the nobility. People compromised with Caesar's young descendant. It was claimed that Livia had been offered as a sacrifice to the monster of proscriptions, with the mission of defending tradition! It might also have been said that this marriage was satisfactory to Octavius' senses, his reason, and his policy. But what about Livia? At the beginning her situation was delicate and uncertain. Delicate, considering the circumstances of the marriage; it was a fine opportunity for gossip – 'In Rome fortunate people have children in three months' – uncertain, since at that time Octavius was far from ruling the world. In precarious health, Caesar's heir proved himself a mediocre general. The glory of battles, the defeat of the republicans, these were the adornments of Antony: Octavia was the woman who seemed destined for a fine future. To foresee Augustus at the time of Octavius Caesar's marriage to Livia was truly premature. It is not known, besides, whether Livia accepted this union willingly; but it was traditional in great families to sacrifice feeling to political convenience. She never failed in this. But she had a more unusual virtue: she knew how to wait.

It was now 38 B.C. Octavius was twenty-five, and he was on his fourth wife; Livia was twenty. Their marriage was to last until death, a half-century later. In fifty years the bonds uniting two people develop considerably, and it is certain that the time was of service to Livia. A great deal of patience was required to see Livia through, from the young wife – interesting for her family background and her beauty but a little mistrusted – who was confronted by the whole tribe of Octavius' relatives, to the dowager empress in whose arms Augustus died and whom he adopted in his will.

Livia knew how to be indispensable. She appeared, however, to be incapable of offering Augustus what was most necessary to him – a son. Livia's character also enters into account. It is not well known. The texts scarcely allow a glimpse of her – or rather, she is a conventional figure like the one representing her on medals, sixty-six years old and looking as if she were twenty; or else it is her enemies who whisper the most monstrous insinuations. Her beauty does seem clear: a regular, rather cold beauty with thin firm lips, and a great distinction of manner without affectation. The adaptibility of her character, perhaps the result of her education, caused her to be called by her great-grandson Caligula, who did not like her, a 'Ulysses in Petticoats.' She possessed to a high degree the combination of qualities which make up good breeding: she was friendly and pleasant without actual warmth, intelligent, refined, and probably very close mouthed, like Octavia. She seems revealed entirely in Seneca's comparison between Livia's attitude and Octavia's, after the death of their sons. In contrast to the deep, inconsolable grief of Octavia, who remained wrapped up in her sorrow until her death, appears the decently limited sorrow of Livia, who accepted the fact, and did not allow it to affect those around her for long. Not to be in the way ... but to be there. In the long run her discreet presence was indispensable. It was all in the manner, in the art of knowing how to propose things, as an obscure rhetorician, copied by Dio Cassius and Seneca, shows so well in speaking of Cinna's conspiracy: 'If you are willing to listen to the remarks of a woman whose fate is bound up with yours and who seeks only your good ...'

At the time of the marriage her fate was still uncertain. Livia devoted herself wholly to her new household, and her children remained with her first husband. Octavius actively prepared a renewal of hostilities against Sextus Pompeius, and suffered serious setbacks on the sea. A meeting took place between Antony, angry at not receiving reinforcements from Italy, and Octavius. Antony came from Greece, crossing to Brundusium. Access to the port was denied him. Furious, he landed at Tarentum, where Octavius came to see him. Relations were strained between the two men. Octavia served as mediator, taking the first great feminine role; for she was truly the connecting link between her husband and her brother. Tradition has echoed it: in the presence of Maecenas and Agrippa she urged her brother not to make the happiest of women the most wretched. 'I shall

be miserable without redress: on whatsoever side victory falls, I shall be the loser!'

Poor Octavia – this was to be her last fair season! Destiny was against her after this false reconciliation at Tarentum, where she obtained from her brother a thousand men for her husband, and from her husband twenty brigantines for her brother. Not only was the struggle inevitable between the two men, but Octavia was to be the pretext for it. She left for Syria with her husband, but from Corcyra Antony sent his wife and all his children back to Italy. He never came back to Rome.

In 36 B.C. Octavius had finished with Sextus Pompeius and with Lepidus, least mentioned of the triumvirs. Octavius received tribunal powers and was made sacrosanct. The following year, Octavia and Livia both received the same privilege and were emancipated at the same time. The two women were on the same level; the two men began not to be . . . . Antony led a large expedition against the Parthians, but he had never received the troops promised by Octavius at Tarentum, and in 35 B.C. Octavius actually refused them again. Octavia then asked to set sail and join her husband; and Plutarch has a cruel sentence: '. . . He gave her leave, not so much, say most authors, to gratify his sister, as to obtain a fair pretence to begin the war afresh upon her dishonorable reception . . .' And so she left, provided with all the gifts which might please her husband: two thousand picked men, very well equipped with arms as fine as the praetorian guard, a provision of clothing for the soldiers, pack animals, money, and considerable presents for his officers and friends. But she did not get far: upon arriving in Athens, she received letters from her husband enjoining her to wait him there, and then sending her back to Italy. He was waiting for twenty thousand men – and he had Cleopatra.

After this frustrated journey, this insult, Octavia returned to Rome. Her brother ordered her to leave Antony's house and live alone somewhere else, but she answered that she would not leave her husband's dwelling, and that if he had no other reason for declaring war on Antony, she urged him to forget everything regarding her personally, that it would be dreadful for two great leaders to plunge the Romans into civil war, one for the love of a woman and the other for jealousy. And she lived in her husband's house until a letter of repudiation arrived in Rome and she was driven out of it. This was the elegant origin of the last great Roman war.

Octavius.

That was the end of Octavia's role as wife. From that time on she was only to be the 'sister of the illustrious leader,' as Horace called her in 24 B.C. The sister of the illustrious leader . . . . Just as there could not be two princes, so there could not be two first ladies. Between Livia and Octavia, the struggle thereafter took place in another realm. Does this mean that Livia had a part in this first episode? Certain historians have attributed to her the Machiavellian idea of sending Octavia with presents in order to gain time while Octavius made preparations, and in order to bring on the insult which Octavia would not fail to suffer. It is possible; actually nothing is known of it, and from Octavia's point of view it appears natural that she should try to recover her husband and her position. Octavius was the great beneficiary in this affair. The marriage between his sister and Antony had been very useful to his policy, from beginning to end. Events here went beyond individuals.

From then on, the other level on which Octavia and Livia confronted each other was that of maternity. Here Octavia apparently had the advantage, and she was to exploit it. From her two marriages Octavia had five living children: four daughters, two by Marcellus and two by Antony, and one son, Marcellus.

Marlon Brando as Antony in "Julius Caesar".

In addition, she had set her heart on bringing up Antony's children by Fulvia, particularly Julius Antonius, of whom we shall hear more later. Livia had no children by Augustus. The sister of the illustrious leader knew how to bring the blood tie into action: it was Marcellus who married Julia in 25 B.C., and Octavia had a chance to be the mother of an emperor someday. The honors Marcellus received were far out of proportion to his years and appeared to recommend him as the successor to the throne. But it would have been still simpler to act as Caesar had done toward Octavius, and adopt the young man. Then a characteristic reaction occurred: rumors circulated in Rome denouncing the immense honors conferred on this seventeen-year-old boy. Agrippa, laden with much glory and a record of service, left for the East. Maecenas understood Augustus, but he was not on the best of terms with him because of the adultery of his wife Terentia and especially because he did not know how to conceal from his wife her brother Murena's conspiracy. Of Augustus' three customary advisers, only one remained: Livia. She would do everything to prevent this adoption. She had a firm and certain ally in Agrippa. Crafty woman! To whom had she married her son Tiberius, the eldest son of a glorious family? To what famous heiress? To what great name? To the daughter of the plebeian Agrippa and of Pomponia, a knight's daughter. It was most certainly not because of the immense fortune brought as a dowry by Vipsania Agrippina, grand-daughter of the rich banker Atticus; Livia raised Agrippa to her own level, tightening the bonds which should exist between Augustus' wife and his chief counselor and general. Livia thus had an ally against Octavia and Augustus. She flattered Augustus in his republican feelings, which did not exclude ambition. Perhaps, in 23 B.C., Augustus was persuaded that it was better to wait before too clearly designating an heir and giving grounds for being suspected of establishing an hereditary monarchy. Meanwhile, Augustus fell ill, and fearing for his life, he placed his ring on Agrippa's finger . . . .

Once Augustus had recovered, relations between Marcellus and Agrippa became so strained that the latter left for Lesbos. And then Octavia lost her last chance: Marcellus, whose health was delicate, fell ill in his turn. He was under the care of the physician who had saved Augustus a year before, but he died. Octavia was never consoled. She shut herself up

Octavia

Livia.

... to weep and wail; she never accepted the least comforting word, she never allowed herself to seek any distraction. Desiring only obscurity and solitude, even turning away from her brother, she repulsed the poems composed in praise of Marcellus, and closed her ears to all consolation. Keeping away from official ceremonies, loathing the brilliance of her brother's majesty, she buried herself in deep seclusion. Surrounded by her children and grandchildren, she retained until the end her mourning garments, to the great shame of all her relatives, who saw her acting while they still lived as if she were alone in the world ...

This brought to an end the moral and political life of the 'sister of the illustrious leader,' who until then had appeared at all ceremonies at the same time as Livia. She hated all mothers, and particularly Livia, who seemed to steal for her own son the honors which should have devolved on Octavia's. Octavia was to act once more: she intervened in the marriage of Agrippa and

Germanicus.   *Agrippa.*

Julia, as we have already described. Plutarch attributes the idea
of this union to Octavia – rather than see Livia's son marry
Julia, she preferred to take back her daughter Marcella, Agrippa's second wife, so that he might marry Julia. Maecenas was
also to be one of the authors of this marriage. He said to Augustus: 'You have made him so great that you must raise him higher
or destroy him.' And so Livia had to keep her son for another
opportunity. This duel between Livia and Octavia came to an
end in 11 B.C. We are told in a single sentence: the same year
Augustus gave his daughter Julia to Tiberius in marriage and
placed in the vault of the Julii his sister Octavia who had just
died . . . . It only remains to forsake the sorrowful shade of
Augustus' dearly beloved sister. Over this worthy foe, Livia had
won the advantage on all counts.

The struggle was to be more difficult with Augustus' daughter
Julia. In spite of the difference in generations, and although
Julia had been raised by her stepmother in a rather stifling atmos-
phere, Scribonia's daughter seems to have had a less eclipsed

155

personality than Octavia. With her appeared one of the traits characteristic of future women of the family: concern for her position, pride in her lineage. She is summed up in one of the witticisms attributed to her, which serves, though perhaps never actually uttered, to define a personality. When a serious friend of the Emperor tried to persuade her to adopt the simplicity of her father, Julia answered, 'He forgets that he is Caesar, but I remember that I am Caesar's daughter.'

Sole and cherished child of Augustus, she had long known how to employ enough trickery to disarm him. Heiress of her father's whole achievement, either through her husband or her children, she personified the future of the family. For the moment one of the two first ladies of the Roman world, she was sure of one day being the first, and she had the assurance of youth in the face of the preceding generation. At eighteen, when she married her second husband Agrippa, she experienced none of the political difficulties that Livia had already understood at the same age. After her disagreeable childhood under Livia's strict eye and Octavia's mournful gaze, during which she had been kept busy with household tasks and away from contact with the outside world, she had only one thought once she was married: to enjoy the situation. Marcellus was dead – so much the worse for him. She was the one who counted. She married 'old' Agrippa because he was the only one capable of preserving her status in Roman society. Her husband's age and his plebeian crudeness were unimportant: she was Caesar's daughter.

If one is to believe the gossip, she was beautiful, surrounded with admirers; hardly any more is known. 'Her love of letters, her vast knowledge, combined with an agreeable gentleness and a lively wit, a potent feminine charm, bring her admirers of a great variety.' In fact, around Julia gathered a brilliant court composed of all the young nobility in Rome, gilded or not. The greatest personages in the city revolved around her, among others Julius Antonius, Antony's son, whom Octavia had married to her Marcella after the divorce from Agrippa, and Sempronius Gracchus. All these young people, whom the new regime condemned to relative political inactivity, led a life of great style at her court. At the arena where the two first ladies in the empire met, their retinues differed greatly. Around Livia were serious men, with all the weight the Romans attached to the term 'gravis'; as for Julia, she was enthroned amid a flock of luxurious youths.

There is the point. On one side, the puritan aspect – 'old Rome'

– of the new regime, was represented by Livia, who undoubtedly initated it and who was the living example of this moral movement – a woman of the old school, of unimpeachable chastity – unimpeached, at any rate, by historians! Imagine the ridiculous session of the senate at which Augustus, not in the least disturbed by the inconsistency in his words and his actions, declared to the senators: 'It is you who must give advice to your wives and command them, as I do myself!' At these words his audience insisted on learning what advice he gave to Livia. So in spite of himself he spoke about women's clothing and all their finery, and about their comings and goings.

Julia represents the 'scandalous' Rome of the end of the republic. Her popularity undoubtedly came from the fact that she followed the moral tide which Livia was trying to stem. A malevolent tradition dating from Nero's time makes a Messalina out of Julia. But that was probably only a case of projection into the past of an all too recent present. Julia did have lovers and of no mean status. That these fondled in her person their political aspirations is a possibility. For in the end, whether Gracchus or Antonius, Julia's husband would have made a fine match. And there was no law of succession! When Agrippa died, Julia had accomplished her task in vain and given her father three sons. For the competition for her hand was still open, and this time she married a great name, one of the Claudii: Tiberius.

This tardy success for Livia, who compelled her son to this marriage, was only half a victory, since the couple had only one child who died very young. After this misfortune, their misunderstanding led to an actual separation. Julia was reasonably ready to love this husband for whom, it was said, she had had a certain liking during Agrippa's time; but if it did not work, what did she need with Tiberius? She chose her lovers. And there were her sons, spoiled by Augustus who showed them off everywhere, called them princes of youth, and crowned them with honors. The future was theirs.

Powerless and disappointed, Livia could not prevent her son's departure for Rhodes in the year 6 B.C., ostensibly for reasons of health; actually the atmosphere had become intolerable to Tiberius, with a wife of loose morals against whom he dared not act, and her children who were too obviously Augustus' heirs. This seasoned general, for whom a triumph had just been celebrated a year before, felt inferior to the young Caesars. Never had a married woman been freer than Julia: never had a daughter-in-law been so hated by her mother-in-law! While absent, Tiberius' departure was transformed into a partial disgrace; he had to stay on Rhodes against his will. Was Livia then only to be her husband's discreet collaborator, without the power to bring about the return of true Roman nobility for her own children?

As we have already said, her power was considerable. She kept abreast of all affairs, and one year she even seems to have governed Rome, along with Maecenas and Agrippa, in Augustus' absence. She formed the government with these two friends of the Prince; when Maecenas and Agrippa were dead, she remained. Her power is indicated by simple little surface facts; she maintained continuous relations with foreign kings: in 10 B.C. Herod, the king of the Jews, finished building a large city, Caesarea; great celebrations were planned for the inauguration, and Livia sent numerous gifts. When Salome, Herod's sister, had trouble about her marriage, it was to Livia she went for advice. Her epistolary relations were so constant that one of her slaves, Acme, was able to try to help a local conspiracy by falsifying her correspondence. Finally, Livia had protegés for whom she obtained positions: M. Salvius Otho, for example, the Emperor Otho's grandfather of very humble origin, became a senator thanks to her. Galba, another future emperor, even owed her a consulship. These cases are known from the records, but there were certainly many others.

There was nevertheless a domain where Livia's intervention was difficult, and it was the one closest to her heart – family matters. Of course she achieved a great deal for her son, but the supreme power seemed an impossible goal to reach: Augustus' family had an unquestionable priority. The only solution lay in marriages and the uniting of the clans; so Drusus was married to Antonia the Younger, Octavia's last daughter. The marriage between Tiberius and Julia was less easy, and it did not result in a grandson common to Augustus and Livia. Imagine the Empress' fury: to go through so much trouble and arrive at this exile on Rhodes. Julia would pay for this!

The few years following Tiberius' departure were among the most glittering of Augustus' reign. Sumptuous festivities heightened the brilliance of Roman life: the opening of the Forum of Augustus, the dedication of a temple to Mars Ultor. Then suddenly the drama exploded. Augustus was finally made aware of his daughter's transgressions. He was seized with violent anger. He had harbored certain suspicions before, but looking at his grandchildren, who vividly resembled Agrippa, he shunned the thought. He proclaimed that he had two delicate daughters: Julia and the republic. And why this revelation after so many years, at that very moment? Probably because Livia had felt that the time had come to take the chance, and at the point Tiberius had reached, exiled on Rhodes, there was no great risk. The arrogance of Julia's sons was growing as they grew. Livia attacked the weak point: their mother's conduct. She knew how to lead up to the matter, and it provoked a great scandal. Augus-

Julia's sons

tus went to tell his troubles to the senate, and then he hid himself at home. As for Julia, she was deported to a rocky islet off Campania, Pandataria. This was not only a matter of morals: certain of Julia's lovers, like Julius Antonius, were put to death under the accusation of having comitted an offense against the empire, and others were exiled. A fine victory for Livia, indeed, for which the sole responsibility is properly attributed to her.

Despite her popularity, Julia died in exile sixteen years later, in the most complete destitution. Her mother Scribonia, who was with her in her misfortune, was to inform her of the ruin of her family and the accession of Tiberius. Julia had nothing left to do but die, after sixteen years of exile in alternate hope and despair. There were her sons, who interceded in her favor. After three years the people urged the Emperor to recall his daughter: Augustus replied that fire and water would mix before he would determine on that course. Then a quantity of fire was thrown into the Tiber, but nothing came of this trick. Meanwhile they went on pressing the Emperor so hard that Julia was transferred from her island to the mainland.

Livia had no other woman challenging her. Her position was uncontested. Julia's two sons were much affected by their mother's fate. The two daughters came under the rule of their grandmother. Relations were strained. Caius, the eldest of the Caesars, left on a mission to Armenia. The youngest, Lucius, remained mostly in Rome, passing from one mission to another. At eighteen, on his way to Spain, he fell suddenly ill and died. This was in the year 2 A.D. Some time later, Caius, in Armenia, was hit by a nonpoisoned arrow. He was seriously wounded, and he wrote to Rome that he renounced all responsibilities and wished to live as a simple private citizen in Syria. Augustus asked him at least to return to Italy. He set out and died on the way in the year 4 A.D. Julia had no more defenders.

Then Tiberius returned to Rome. Augustus adopted him at the same time as his last grandson, Agrippa Postumus. Livia was soon to reach her goal – it was only necessary to persevere. Between Tiberius and the principate only Agrippa Postumus remained, and after three years it appeared that this young boy was of an unmanageable character. He spent, we are told, the greatest part of his time fishing; what was more, he got angry very quickly. He burst out in abusive language against Livia and in reproaches against Augustus. Since he did not return to a better temper, he was excluded from the imperial family, his property was confiscated for the benefit of the military treasury, and he himself was transported to the island of Planasia. To be sure, this treatment lacked gentleness, and in some measure one might agree with Tacitus' severe judgement: 'Livia had so tyrannized over Augustus' old age that he cast onto the island of Planasia his only grandson Agrippa, who was certainly grossly ignorant and stupidly proud of his physical strength, but innocent of any infamous action.' This was in 7 A.D. It only remained to await events, that is, Augustus' death, while seeing to it that nothing happened on Postumus' side. From then on Tiberius was Augustus' associate as Agrippa had been.

We have come to the decisive period in Livia's life: the time preceding her husband's death. It included the dismal story of Augustus' clandestine visits to his grandson. The sole friend who used to accompany him, Fabius Maximus, committed the indiscretion of mentioning it to his wife Marcia, who had nothing better to do than repeat it to Livia. A short time later Fabius Maximus died, and at his funeral his wife accused herself of bringing on his death . . . . Also a short time later Augustus became ill and died in Livia's arms. Agrippa Postumus was killed; Tiberius had arrived.

Tiberius had left on an expedition to Illyria when he received an urgent letter from his mother, ordering him to return as quickly as possible. It is not known whether he came back to Augustus in time, or if he received the Emperor's last instructions, since Livia had posted guards and took care to hide Augustus' death – allowing time for a tribune to go and execute Agrippa Postumus.

Livia had reigned with her husband, and she had arrived at her son's succession. She has been accused by many ancients and moderns of numerous poisonings, from that of Marcellus to that of Augustus himself, passing through all the Caesars. Leaving Augustus aside, it is certainly true that people died very young in that family, if they were men. Livia's own younger son had also died early – on the battlefield. Postumus' murder being established, it still seems risky to trace them all the way back to Marcellus without further proof. Everyone knows, if only through famous examples, how deceptive coincidence can be. It allows the assertion of guilt no more than that of innocence.

Tiberius' accession, against Augustus will, was a certainty, thanks to his mother. Augustus would gladly have designated

Germanicus, Livia's grandson through Drusus. He was satisfied, we are told, to be conquered by. his wife's prayers, and have Tiberius adopt Germanicus even though Tiberius already had a son of his own. There was Livia, thereafter 'Augusta' by her husband's will in which she was adopted and brought into the family. On her son, who was incidentally a man of fifty-five, or rather on Rome, the influence of this 'Augusta' was so extensive that Tiberius was jealous of it. But he could only confirm his helplessness; and Livia had fifteen more years to live!

She was made his partner in power, because Tiberius could not do otherwise, holding it as he did through her. Besides, she was unquestionably a help to him, and Tiberius often asked her advice. But discord was not long in arising, since she had more authority than he. For another thing, her character became more and more imperious as she aged. So Tiberius spaced out meetings with her, avoided long secret discussions, and then warned Livia not to involve herself in important matters which were not suitable for women. He censured her interference, when a fire broke out near the Temple of Vesta and in person she had exhorted the people and soldiers to bring help, as she had done in her husband's time. Their lack of harmony became public, and in 26 A.D. Tiberius finally shut himself up on Capri. In all personal affairs Livia remained the court of highest appeal; her protection was the most effective, and so was her hatred.

Among her victims may be counted the poet Ovid and the younger Julia. Her own grandson Germanicus should also be included, who with Agrippina the Elder formed the couple designed to succeed Tiberius. Through hatred of this woman, Livia allowed Agrippina's family to suffer actual persecution.

Livia died in the year 29, at the age, canonical for the period, of eighty-six, to the great relief of Tiberius who was at last alone. He himself was seventy years old!

The continuation and end of our story gravitate around another outstanding individual, the Empress Agrippina, who knew her great-grandmother Livia in childhood.

The will to power, the patient and constant pursuit of the ambitious goal she had set herself were characteristic of Agrippina the Younger. Her generation was born to the purple; her ancestors were illustrious, and people delighted in extolling her background: she effectively combined direct descent from Augustus through her mother, the elder Agrippina, and from Livia and Octavia through her father Germanicus. The dreamt-of union between the families of Livia and Augustus was accomplished in her. She had always lived in the society of the

AGRIPPINA.

principate, the creation of which had occurred before her birth. It was the time of her great-grandfather Augustus that saw her earliest years, and her childhood unfolded in the midst of deference, close to power, among escorts, hearing talk of the succession and the right of the empire. Aware of the difficulties of the imperial family, she understood the opportunities of well-directed ambition and the risks involved in making mistakes.

The example not to follow was provided by her mother Agrippina, called the Elder: a fine story of a frustrated life, in spite of magnificent chances. Germanicus, Tiberius' adoptive son, had appeared as his designated successor since before Augustus' death. The couple's numerous offspring – three sons and three daughters – seemed to assure the succession for this branch of the family, which finally brought about the union of the Julii and the Claudii. To say that everything was ruined through the fault of Agrippina the Elder would doubtless not be far from the truth. She multiplied her mistakes. Completely lacking in political talent, unable to hide her feelings, she had boundless confidence in her high lineage and in the unusual popularity which she owed as much to herself as to her husband. We have already been able to appreciate to what extent, in the course of her travels, she had the sense of popular contact. An emperor like Tiberius, who lacked it, and who liked meek women, was a trying circumstance. Although Tiberius had to give way before Livia, he intended to remain master in regard to his daughter-in-law and niece.

In addition, Agrippina had two enemies, Livia and Livilla. With her grandmother the animosity was of long standing: it came from hostility between a fiery personality and a sad step-child without a real mother. With Livilla, Germanicus' sister, it was a matter of rivalry between two young women equal in birth, almost equal in their marriages, whose husbands might nourish ambitions that were also equal. Agrippina nevertheless had the advantage . . . until Germanicus' catastrophic death.

She remained convinced of the Emperor's responsibility in her husband's death. She proclaimed it throughout a city which asked nothing more than to spread rumors of poisonings and assassinations. When she returned to Rome, after a married life of nothing but travel and glory, Tiberius had to say to her: 'You think yourself injured if you are not in command.' Germanicus' friends gathered about her; for them the General's death had taken on all the attraction of disaster. Agrippina became the standard-bearer of the malcontents and of an opposition which would not have dared to show itself at the end of Augustus' reign. Tiberius' age certainly justified hopes, but the Emperor had a son, Drusus, who was clearly designated as his successor; and Agrippina's oldest son was only fourteen when Germanicus died!

It was then that Sejanus' formidable ambition made its appearance. With Tiberius this knight doubtless wished to repeat, only in better terms, the story of Augustus and Agrippa. Despite difficulties Sejanus had been able to gain Tiberius' confidence, the emperor was glad to call him partner in his work, not only in conversation but in the senate and before the people. Drusus, of passionate temperament and unable to countenance a rival, showed his fist to Sejanus during a chance argument, and hit him in the face. Some time later, Drusus fell sick and died.

The inevitable result was that Agrippina's two elder sons were proposed as heirs. Having become the center of attention, Agrippina fell into all the traps Sejanus set for her. Her ambition and her hopes lacked discretion. Her followers aggravated her pride further by suggesting that she was not being shown enough consideration. The whole family had no trouble arraying itself against her. Still more troublesome was the discord she provoked between her two sons by obviously preferring the elder.

We may allow this wind of discord to blow through the imperial family, over Livia, Livilla, Agrippina and her sons – this gust so cleverly stirred up and directed by Sejanus: we are coming to worse extremities. Not, however, before Livia's death. It was enough to spy on Agrippina and her eldest son and to exacerbate their natural arrogance. Perhaps it would bear watching . . . .

It lasted until the day when Tiberius, from Capri, addressed a letter to the senate, 'full of spleen, in which he heaped up shameful accusations.' In fact, the insolence of Agrippina's utterances and her rebellion constituted the main point of the accusation. There was amazement and noise in Rome. A second letter reprimanded the people and the senate. A charge of *lèse-majesté* was laid against Agrippina and her eldest son Nero, and they were condemned to banishment. Her second son was also arrested and imprisoned in a dungeon under the palace. All three were not long in dying, in horrible fashion.

The younger Agrippina drew the moral from this tragic story, which she recounts in detail in her memoirs: it is necessary to

Agrippina the Elder.
Agrippina the Younger.

know how to dissimulate, like Livia, to wait, and then, at the right moment, to act without scruple.

This shrewd princess escaped the family persecution in 28 A.D. by marrying her cousin Domitius Ahenobarbus, who bore one of the greatest names in Roman aristocracy. Her two younger sisters were to be less lucky than she, and had to wait a long time, at home with their grandmother Antonia the Younger, for the husbands of simple origin whom Tiberius would provide for them. The success of this marriage does not seem to have been remarkable, and when a son was born, the future Nero, Domitius Ahenobarbus replied to his friends' congratulations by saying that nothing could be born of Agrippina and himself except what was detestable and fatal to the state.

Times had changed. It was the youngest and only surviving brother of Agrippina the Younger who had just ascended the throne when this little boy was born: it was Caligula whom Agrippina asked to give a name to her son at the time of his purification. For a joke, Caligula looked at his uncle Claudius, the laughingstock of the court, and said: 'His name!' Agrippina scorned it. Had not an astrologer predicted before the child's birth that he would succeed to the empire and cause the death of his mother? Carried away, the latter had exclaimed 'Let him kill me, so long as he reigns!'

There is no doubt that Agrippina, like her sister, lent herself to Caligula's fancies. But his favorite was Drusilla, whom her brother publicly treated as his wife, after he had stolen her from her husband. In 40, Domitius Ahenobarbus died, and Caligula took this opportinuty to accuse Agrippina of adultery and treason. He had her deported, and confiscated her whole inheritance; her life was even threatened. Fortunately for her, Caligula's assassination and the accession of Uncle Claudius reversed the situation again. Agrippina was immediately recalled to Rome and reinstated. It was probably then that she vainly made advances to Galba, and then, to gild her escutcheon, married a man who was obscure but extremely rich: Crispus Passienus. Besides, he died almost immediately.

We have come to the period of Messalina's reign. There seems

Caligula and Drusilla.
Claudius.

to be general agreement: the Emperor Claudius, not without intelligence but characterless and totally lacking in prestige, was the plaything of his wives and freedmen. To be in favor at court, it was thus necessary to make an ally of a freedman; and in the case of a woman, it was also necessary to avoid Messalina's wrath, for she was jealous of all power and envious of all beauty and wealth. Agrippina had to protect herself against the cruelty and jealousy of her aunt. It was a purely feminine rivalry, but when a woman was her adversary, Messalina used every means of getting rid of her. Assassins entered Nero's room one day, but the legend tells how they were terrified by a snake which rose up beside the child's bed. It was no easier to do away with his mother, whose virtue for the moment was foolproof. In addition, Messalina's ideas lacked continuity; she passed from one caprice to another. Her last lover, Silius, cost her her life, since Claudius' freedmen preferred keeping their master to having Messalina and Silius in his place. The execution was their work, even before Claudius could react.

With Messalina dead, a real contest began among all the women aspiring to the signal honor of being empress. The chief ones among them had each been able to win over, by every possible means, one of the Emperor's favorite freedmen:

> The destruction of Messalina shook the Imperial house; for a strife arose among the freedmen, who should choose a wife for Claudius, impatient as he was of a single life and submissive to the rule of wives. The ladies were fired with no less jealousy. Each insisted on her rank, beauty and fortune, and pointed to her claims to such a marriage. But the keenest competition was between Lollia Paulina, the daughter of Marcus Lollius, an ex-consul, and Julia Agrippina, the daughter of Germanicus. Callistus favoured the first, Pallas the second. Aelia Paetina however . . . had the support of Narcissus. The Emperor, who inclined now one way, now another, as he listened to this or that adviser, summoned the disputants to a conference and bade them express their opinions and give their reasons . . . . Narcissus dwelt on the marriage of years gone by, on the tie of offspring, for Paetina was the mother of Antonia, and on the advantage of excluding a new element from his household, by the return of a wife to whom he was accustomed, and who would assuredly not look with a stepmother's animosity on Britannicus and Octavia, who were next

169

"We have come to the period of Messalina's reign."
(Maria Felix in "Messalina").

in her affections to her own children. Callistus argued that she was compromised by her long separation, and that were she to be taken back, she would be supercilious on the strength of it. It would be far better to introduce Lollia, for, as she had no children of her own, she would be free from jealousy, and would take the place of a mother towards her stepchildren . . . . Pallas again selected Agrippina for special commendation because she would bring with her Germanicus' grandson, who was thoroughly worthy of Imperial rank, the scion of a noble house and a link to unite the descendants of the Claudian family. He hoped that a woman who was the mother of many children and still in the freshness of youth, would not carry off the grandeur of the Caesars to some other house . . . . This advice prevailed, backed up as it was by Agrippina's charms. On the pretext of her relationship, she paid frequent visits to her uncle, and so won his heart that she was preferred to the others, and, though not yet his wife, already possessed a wife's power . . .

So Agrippina triumphed, Tacitus tells us, thanks to her family relationship with her future husband, and in spite of the fact that this tie could represent an obstacle to the marriage. It was child's play to have the senate pass a law allowing an uncle to marry his niece. Thanks to Pallas, but also to herself, she was empress in 49 A.D.

From that point on the path seemed easy. She had only to oust Britannicus, the son of Claudius, for the benefit of her own. What is a child, when one has the assurance and authority of a wife who is sure of her husband? Young Nero's rise was slow but sure: the broken engagement of Claudius' daughter Octavia to his advantage, afterwards marriage; and then from son-in-law he soon became adoptive son.

While she was arranging the future for her son, the mother thrust aside every rival and fought against every influence other than her own. Woe betide those women who might be pleasing to Claudius! Agrippina knew her husband's weakness only too well. She ruined a noble lady, Calpurnia, because the Prince had praised her beauty, quite by chance in conversation and not through love. Against Lollia Paulina, who was her mortal enemy ever since their matrimonial rivalry, Agrippina sought weapons and an accuser. Lollia was blamed for the Chaldeans, the soothsayers, and for the questions asked the oracle of Apollo at

Claros on the subject of the Emperor's marriage. Without giving the defendant a hearing, Claudius took the floor in the senate and, after a long exordium on her nobility, affirmed that this woman's schemes were harmful to the state, and that it was necesserry to prevent her crimes from being committed. She was exiled, and of all her immense fortune she was left only five million sesterces. And Agrippina sent her a tribune who forced her to take her own life.

It was not enough to eliminate the women. She also had to defend herself from the fréedmen. Pallas remained devoted to her, but Narcissus opposed her in every way, and the conflicts between them were often violent. Narcissus was responsible for Messalina's death, and rumors began to circulate: had not Claudius one day declared, in a state bordering on drunkenness, that fate desired all his wives to be unchaste but not unpunished? Did he not have sudden outbursts of affection for Britannicus, who was now a man? Agrippina's uneasiness grew, and the illness which carried off Narcissus spurred her to action. Tacitus gives a famous account of Claudius' murder:

> Thereupon Agrippina deliberated on the nature of the poison to be used. The deed would be betrayed by one that was sudden and instantaneous, while if she chose a slow and lingering poison, there was a fear that Claudius, when near his end, might, on detecting the treachery, return to his love for his son. She decided on some rare compound which might derange him and delay his death. A person skilled in such matters was selected, Locusta by name, who had lately been condemned for poisoning, and had long been retained as one of the tools of despotism. By this woman's art the poison was prepared, and it was to be administered by a eunuch, who was accustomed to bring in and taste the dishes . . . the poison was infused into some mushrooms, a favourite delicacy, and its effect not at the instant perceived, from the Emperor's lethargic, or intoxicated condition. His bowels too were relieved and this seemed to have saved him. Agrippina was thoroughly dismayed. Fearing the worst, and defying the immediate obloquy of the deed, she availed herself of the complicity of Xenophon, the physician, which she had already secured. Under pretence of helping the Emperor's efforts to vomit, this man, it is supposed, introduced into his throat a feather smeared with some rapid poison; for he knew that

the greatest crimes are perilous in their inception, but well rewarded after their consummation . . . . Meanwhile though the Senate was summoned, and prayers rehearsed by the consuls and priests for the Emperors recovery, though the lifeless body was being wrapped in blankets with warm applications, all was being arranged to establish Nero on the throne. At first Agrippina, seemingly overwhelmed by grief and seeking comfort, clasped Britannicus in her embraces, called him the very image of his father, and hindered him by every possible device from leaving the chamber. She also detained his sisters, Antonia and Octavia, closed every approach to the palace with a military guard, and repeatedly gave out that the Emperor's health was better, so that the soldiers might be encouraged to hope, and that the fortunate moment foretold by the astrologers might arrive . . . . At last, at noon on the 13th of October, the gates of the palace were suddenly thrown open, and Nero, accompanied by Burrus, went forth to the cohort which was on guard after military custom. There, at the suggestion of the commanding officer, he was hailed with joyful shouts, and set on a litter. Some it is said, hesitated, and looked round and asked where Britannicus was; then when there was no one to lead a resistance, they yielded to what was offered them. Nero was conveyed into the camp and having first spoken suitably to the occasion and promised a donative after the example of his father's bounty, he was unanimously greeted as Emperor . . . . Divine honors were decreed to Claudius, and his funeral rites were solemnized on the same scale as those of Augustus; for Agrippina strove to emulate the magnificence of her great-grandmother, Livia . . .

The first part of the astrologer's prediction had come true: Agrippina's son reigned. The mother was soon to consider the second part – death.

At the beginning of Nero's reign, Agrippina's assurance and authority were still increasing. She could eliminate all the contrary influences which hung over Claudius. For the moment, the extremely young Nero let her do what she wanted. The marks of honor and power were freely granted to her.

But difficulties were not long in arising: opposition first came from Nero's two preceptors, Seneca and Burrus. A woman's authority antagonized them, all the more because each of them owed her a great deal. But the greatest danger came from Agrippina herself. The undeniable political sense and the intelligence of this woman vanished in the presence of her son. For her, he remained a difficult child. She never admitted that he might have become a man. She instructed him, corrected him, commanded him. She could only play the imperious mother. And so her strictness caused her to lose the fruits of her labors.

Nero fell in love with a freedwoman, Actë.

> . . . Agrippina, however, raved with a woman's fury about having a freedwoman for a rival, a slave girl for a daughter-in-law . . . . The fouler her reproaches, the more powerfully did they inflame him, till completely mastered by the strength of his desire, he threw off all respect for his mother, and put himself under the guidance of Seneca . . . . Then Agrippina, changing her tactics, plied the lad with various blandishments, and even offered the seclusion of her chamber for the concealment of indulgences which youth and the highest rank might claim. She went further; she pleaded guilty to an ill-timed strictness, and handed over to him the abundance of her wealth, which nearly approached the Imperial treasures, and from having been of late extreme in her restraint of her son, became now, on the other hand, lax to excess. The change did not escape Nero . . .

From then on, understanding between mother and son showed itself to be impossible, and Agrippina seemed to lose all notion of reality:

> . . . Agrippina rushed into frightful menaces, sparing not the prince's ears her solemn protest 'that Britannicus was now of full age, he who was the true and worthy heir of his father's sovereignty, which a son, by mere admission and adoption, was abusing in outrages on his mother . . . . With her stepson she would go to camp, where on one side should be heard the daughter of Germanicus; on the other, the crippled Burrus and the exile Seneca, claiming, forsooth, with disfigured hand, and a pedant's tongue, the government of the world.'

This imprudence of Agrippina cost Britannicus his life. She realized with terror that there was actually no longer anything for which her son envied her! For the first time, Agrippina was brought to the point of defending her life:

173

BRITANNICUS:
LATEST VERSIONS

Jean Marais.
Marie Bell.
Marguerite Jamois.
Yvernel.
Renée Faure.
Roland Alexandre.

... Nero ordered the departure of the military guard now kept for the Emperor's mother as it had formerly been for the Imperial consort ... He also gave her a separate establishment ... In a moment Agrippina's doors were deserted; there was no one to comfort or to go near her, except a few ladies, whether out of love or malice was doubtful. One of these was Junia Silana, whom Messalina had driven from her husband, Caius Silius .... Conspicuous for her birth, her beauty, and her wantonness, she had long been a special favourite of Agrippina, till after a while there were mutual dislikes .... Silana having now a prospect of vengeance, suborned as accusers two of her creatures ... with a hint that it was Agrippina's purpose to encourage in revolutionary designs Rubellius Plautus, who on his mother's side was as nearly connected as Nero with the Divine Augustus ...

This story was recounted to Nero by Paris, an actor and freedman of Domitia, Nero's aunt: between Domitia and Agrippina there existed an implacable jealousy. The Emperor's first impulse was to put Plautus and his mother to death: 'Nero, in his bewilderment and impatience to destroy his mother, could not be put off till Burrus answered for her death, should she be convicted of the crime ...' But there were no accusers, and Agrippina, in the presence of Burrus, Seneca, and of 'freedmen charged with observing the interview' – Agrippina, who, Tacitus tells us, 'had not forgotten her pride' – succeeded in warding off the suspicions. By means of a haughty and aggressive 'speech for the defense ... she obtained vengeance on her accusers.'

But the Empress' position became impossible to hold when Nero fell in love with Poppaea. This was no freedwoman. 'This woman had everything – glory, beauty, fortune, wit – except a right mind. Her manner was modest, her morals lax. She made no distinction between her husband and her lovers.' She allowed herself to be seduced by the youth and elegance of Otho, although she was married to a knight, 'and also because of the reputation he had as a favorite of Nero. The adultery was soon followed by marriage.'

There are many versions of Poppaea's conquest of Nero. Had the captivated Emperor consigned her to Otho on trust until he had got rid of Octavia? Had Otho committed an annoying imprudence or cherished an immoral ambition? 'Otho now began to praise his wife's beauty and accomplishments to the

Emperor, either from a lover's thoughtlessness or to inflame Nero's passion in the hope of adding to his own influence by the further tie which would arise out of possession of the same woman . . .'

But it is always Poppaea's coquetry which captures Nero:

Once having gained admission, Poppaea won her way by artful blandishments, pretending that she could not resist her passion and that she was captivated by Nero's person. Soon, as the Emperor's love grew ardent, she would change and be supercilious and, if she were detained more than one or two nights, would say again and again that she was a married woman and could not give up her husband attached as she was to Otho by a manner of life, which no one equalled . . .

The mistress' ambition was now to become the wife. But there was Octavia . . . and Agrippina. The latter was naturally opposed to the repudiation of Claudius' daughter without reason. The scandal would be too great. Did Agrippina then conceive the idea of seducing Nero? Here is what Dio Cassius says:

. . . Did the thing actually occur or was it rather a slander to which the behavior of Agrippina and Nero gave rise? I could not say. I will report a well known fact, which is that Nero dearly loved a courtesan because of her resemblance to Agrippina. Whenever he enjoyed her or boasted of her to his friends, he recalled his mother!

Poppaea soon understood that she would never become Empress as long as her lover's mother lived. Nero surrendered to her threats and supplications; he ordered this murder, certainly the most horrible of all, the culmination of a long history of crime and deadly foreboding. Did it not herald the murderer's own death? Did it not sound the knell of the Julio-Claudian dynasty? But here is Tacitus for the last time: 'At last . . . he resolved to destroy her . . . merely deliberating whether it was to be accomplished by poison, or by the sword or by any other violent means. Poison at first seemed best . . .' But how to administer it? And Agrippina:

had fortified her constitution by the use of antidotes. How again the dagger and its work were to be kept secret, no one could suggest . . . An ingenious suggestion was offered by Anicetus . . . He explained that a vessel could be constructed, from which a part might by a contrivance be detached, when out at sea, so as to plunge her unawares into the water. 'Nothing,' he said, 'allowed of accidents so much as the sea, and should she be overtaken by shipwreck, who would be so unfair as to impute to crime an offence committed by the winds and waves?' . . . He enticed his mother (to Baiae) wishing thus to spread a rumour of reconciliation . . . Here was a vessel distinguished from others by its equipment, seemingly meant, among other things, to do honor to his mother . . . Agrippina had heard of the plot, and in doubt whether she was to believe it, was conveyed to Baiae in her litter. There some soothing words allayed her fear; she was graciously received, and seated at table above the Emperor. Nero prolonged the banquet with various conversation, passing from a youth's playful familiarity to an air of constraint, which seemed to indicate serious thought, and then, after protracted festivity, escorted her on her departure, clinging with kisses to her eyes and bosom, either to crown his hypocrisy or because the last sight of a mother on the eve of destruction caused a lingering pang even in that brutal heart.

The night was starry, the sea calm, the vessel set sail and was wrecked as planned. But, in the general uproar, owing to the sacrifice of one of her ladies, Acerronia, who cried out in the midst of the confusion that she was Agrippina, and was knocked senseless by blows from the oars and boathooks, the Empress was able to save herself by swimming to shore.

She had herself carried to her villa, and there she realized '. . . that her only safeguard against treachery was to ignore it. Then she sent her freedman Agerinus to tell her son how by heaven's favour and his good fortune she had escaped a terrible disaster . . .'

Nero learned that his mother was safe.

Then, paralysed with terror and protesting that she would show herself the next moment eager for vengeance . . . he asked what recourse he had against all this . . . that Nero must perish unless Agrippina were at once crushed . . . . Anicetus, without a pause, claimed for himself the consummation of the crime. At those words, Nero declared that that day gave him empire ... Meantime, Agrippina's peril being universally known and taken to be an accidental occurrence, a vast multitude streamed to the spot with torches, and as soon as all knew that she was safe, they at once prepared to wish her joy, till the sight of an armed and threatening force scared them away. Anicetus then surrounded the house with a guard, and having burst open the gates, dragged off the slaves who met him, till he came to the door of her chamber ... A small lamp was in the room, and one slave-girl with Agrippina, who grew more and more anxious ... and looking round saw Anicetus, who had with him the captain of the trireme, Herculaius, and Obaritus, a centurion of marines .... The assassins closed in round her couch, and the captain of the trireme first struck her head violently with a club. Then, as the centurion bared his sword for the fatal deed, presenting her person, she exclaimed, 'Smite my womb,' and with many wounds she was slain.

The Imperial Family

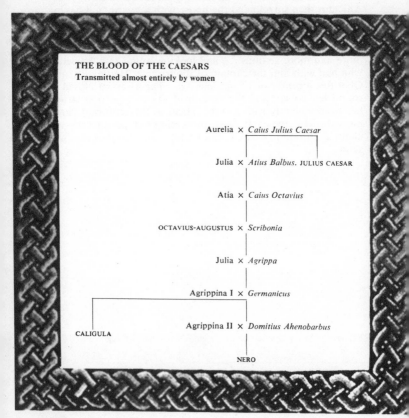

THE BLOOD OF THE CAESARS
Transmitted almost entirely by women

Aurelia × *Caius Julius Caesar*

Julia × *Atius Balbus*. JULIUS CAESAR

Atia × *Caius Octavius*

OCTAVIUS-AUGUSTUS × *Scribonia*

Julia × *Agrippa*

Agrippina I × *Germanicus*

CALIGULA

Agrippina II × *Domitius Ahenobarbus*

NERO

THE SEARCH FOR MALE HEIRS
The practice and the usefulness of adoption

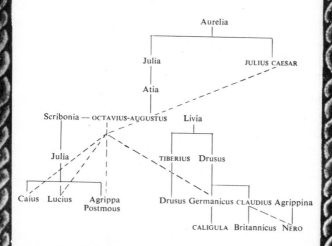

The diagonal dotted lines indicate adoption.

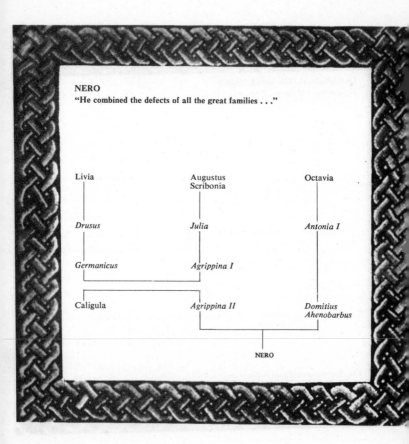

NERO
"He combined the defects of all the great families . . ."

Livia	Augustus Scribonia	Octavia
Drusus	*Julia*	*Antonia I*
Germanicus	*Agrippina I*	
Caligula	*Agrippina II*	*Domitius Ahenobarbus*
	NERO	

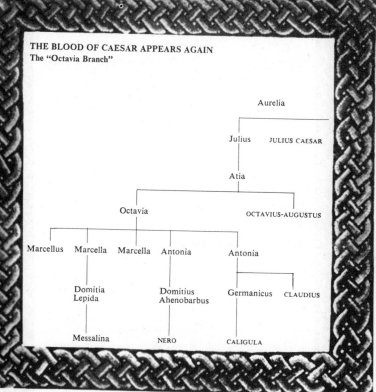

THE BLOOD OF CAESAR APPEARS AGAIN
The "Octavia Branch"

THE SUCCESSION OF AUGUSTUS

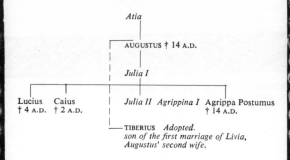

Atia

AUGUSTUS † 14 A.D.

Julia I

| Lucius † 4 A.D. | Caius † 2 A.D. | | *Julia II* | *Agrippina I* | Agrippa Postumus † 14 A.D. |

TIBERIUS   *Adopted. son of the first marriage of Livia, Augustus' second wife.*

THE SUCCESSION OF TIBERIUS

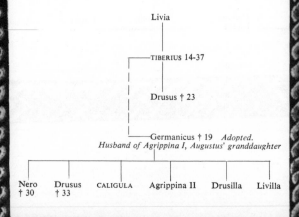

Livia

TIBERIUS 14-37

Drusus † 23

Germanicus † 19   *Adopted. Husband of Agrippina I, Augustus' granddaughter*

| Nero † 30 | Drusus † 33 | CALIGULA | Agrippina II | Drusilla | Livilla |

THE SUCCESSION OF CALIGULA

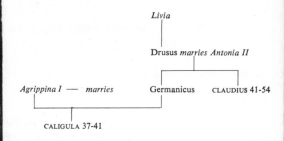

Livia

Drusus *marries Antonia II*

Agrippina I — *marries* — Germanicus   CLAUDIUS 41-54

CALIGULA 37-41

THE SUCCESSION OF CLAUDIUS

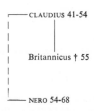

CLAUDIUS 41-54

Britannicus † 55

NERO 54-68

Adopted. Son of a first marriage of
Agrippina II, Claudius' second wife
and Augustus' great-granddaughter.

Chronological Table

41	Division of the Roman world among the triumvirs. Fulvia creates trouble for Octavius: the Perugian war. Antony falls in love with Cleopatra.
40	Peace of Brundusium: compromise between Octavius and Antony. Marriage of Octavia and Antony.
39	Marriage of Octavius and Scribonia, followed by the birth of Octavius' only child: Julia.
38	Repudiation of Scribonia, marriage of Octavius and Livia.
31	Repudiation of Octavia. Antony is still in love with Cleopatra. Battle of Actium.
30	Death of Antony and Cleopatra.

The Foundation of The Empire

27	Octavius take the surname Augustus.
25	Julia marries Marcellus.
21	Julia marries Agrippa, friend and associate of Augustus.
18	Laws concerning marriage and adultery.
17	Augustus adopts the sons of Agrippa and Julia.
12	Death of Agrippa.
11	Marriage of Julia and Tiberius.
6	Tiberius in exile on Rhodes.
2	Exile of Julia.

THE CHRISTIAN ERA

2	Death of Lucius Caesar.
4	Death of Caius Caesar. Unrest and disorder: conspiracy of Cinna. Recall of Tiberius.
9	Law concerning sterile marriages.
14	Death of Augustus, founder of the new regime.

The Julio-Claudian Dynasty
The descendants of Livia, Octavia and Julia are:

Tiberius 14-37
He continues the work of his father-in-law, apparently with conscientiousness.

14-16	Germanicus in Germany
17-19	Journey of Agrippina I and Germanicus in the East. Death of Germanicus.

23	Death of Drusus, son of Tiberius, perhaps poisoned by his wife Livilla on the instigation of Sejanus.
26	Tiberius leaves for Capri, to escape Rome and his mother.
29	Death of Livia. Agrippina I and her son Nero are banished.
30	Drusus, another son of Agrippina and Germanicus, is imprisoned.
31	Fall and death of Sejanus, thanks to Antonia's letter denouncing his intrigues.
37	Solitary death of Tiberius.

Caligula 37-41
He is the sole surviving son of Germanicus. He establishes the imperial authority in Oriental fashion. His relations with his sister Drusilla cause fear of an incestuous marriage.

| 41 | Assassination of Caligula. |

Claudius 51-54
The Emperor is found by the soldiers who straggle through the palace at the time of Caligula's execution. He transforms the empire into a bureaucratic monarchy, through a whole series of administrative reforms.

41-48	Messalina empress.
49	Marriage of Agrippina II and Claudius.
50	Agrippina causes the adoption of her son Nero.
53	Marriage of Octavia, daughter of Claudius, and Nero.
54	Poisoning of Claudius.

Nero 54-68

55	Poisoning of Britannicus.
59	Death of Agrippina by order of her son.
62	Death of Octavia, wife of Nero. Marriage of Nero and Poppaea.
64	Burning of Rome.
65	Death of Poppaea.
68	Death of Nero.

Selected Bibliography

For those who would like to know more about this history, two kinds of reading may be suggested: the ancient texts and contemporary works.

The ancient texts, which have been freely quoted here, refer to the following authors:

TACITUS. *The Complete Works*. Translated by A. J. CHURCH and W. J. BRODRIBB. Modern Library.
This is the most complete and the most thrilling history there is. Tacitus likes to dwell on the defects of the imperial regime.

SUETONIUS. *The Twelve Caesars*. Translated by ROBERT GRAVES. Penguin Classics.
Only the first six lives. These monographs on the emperors include a quantity of detail about current affairs, but they show an excessive taste for the scandalous anecdote.

JUVENAL. *Satires*. Translated by G. G. RAMSAY. Loeb Classical Library.
Satire VI, in particular, is devoted to women. The literary form of these works demands a certain virulence which is quite in accordance with the Roman spirit.

OVID. *The Art of Love*. Translated by J. H. MOZLEY. Loeb Classical Library. *Amores*. Translated by GRANT SHOWERMAN. Loeb Classical Library.
We have quoted at length from these works, which seem indicative of the mentality of the age.

HORACE. *Satires*. Translated by H. R. FAIRCLOUGH. Loeb Classical Library. *Odes and Epodes*. Translated by C. E. BENNETT. Loeb Classical Library.
Horace was one of the official poets.

MARTIAL. *Epigrams*. Translated by WALTER C. A. KER. 2 vols. Loeb Classical Library.
Martial wrote around fifty years after the period studied here, in spiteful mockery of his contemporaries.

There are allusions to the subjects we have dealt with in many other Latin authors, but it is not possible to list them all here.

Among the texts which are relevant to an understanding of the mentality of the preceding epoch, the following might be suggested: The letters of CICERO, and the works of the poets CATULLUS and PROPERTIUS.

Greek authors may also be consulted:

189

PLUTARCH. *The Lives of the Noble Grecians and Romans*. Translated by JOHN DRYDEN. Modern Library.
He gives a whole series of particulars about Octavia, in the life of Antony.

DIO CASSIUS. *Roman History*. Translated by E. CARY. 9 vols. Loeb Classical Library.
He recounts the history of Rome year by year with many details.

The contemporary works allow an ultimately more thorough study of each subject. Almost all the books on this limited list give complementary bibliographical material.

An intimate presentation of the most important great Roman ladies is given in biographical form in:

FERRERO, G. *The Women of the Caesars*. New York and London: 1925.

FRIEDLANDER, L. *Darstellungen aus der Sittengeschichte Roms in der Zeit von Augustus bis zum Ausgang der Antonius.*

Some books which give the atmosphere of the period:

MARROU, H. I. *A History of Education in Antiquity*. Translated by GEORGE LAMB. New York: 1956.

CARCOPINO, J. *Daily Life in Ancient Rome*. Translated by E. O. LORIMER. New Haven: 1940.
The period dealt with is slightly later than that of this book.

For a complete picture of the time of the great Roman ladies, the following may be consulted:

MOMMSEN, T. *The History of Rome*. Translated by W. P. DICKSON. 4 vols. (Everyman Edition) London and New York: 1929-31.

ROSTOVTZEFF, M. *The Social and Economic History of the Roman Empire*. 2 vols. (2nd ed.) Oxford, 1957.

FERRERO, G. *Characters and Events of Roman History from Caesar to Nero*. Translated by F. L. FERRERO. New York and London: 1909.

COOK, S. A., ADCOCK, F. E., CHARLESWORTH, M. P., (eds.) *The Augustan Empire, B.C. 44 – A.D. 70*. Cambridge Ancient History Vol. X. Cambridge and New York: 1934.

SYME, R. *The Roman Revolution*. Oxford, 1939.

CARY, M. and others (eds). *The Oxford Classical Dictionary*. Oxford, 1949.

PAULY WISSOWA. *Real-Encyclopadie der klass. Altertumswissenschaft*. Stuttgart, 1894-1919.
In the process of being re-edited and completed. Most of the women we have mentioned have biographical notes accompanied by scholarly critical apparatus.

Sources

MOSAICS

Fragment of pavement from the Aventine. Vatican Museum.
Detail of a mosaic from the Baths of Caracalla.

STATUES

Museo delle Terme. Rome.
(left) Greek statue. Naples Museum. (right) Roman statue. Vatican Museum. Rome.
Museo dei Conservatori. Rome.
Museo delle Terme. Rome.
Palatine Hill.
Capitoline Museum. Rome.
Temple of Rome and Augustus. Ostia Antica.
The House of the Vestals. The Forum. Rome.
Museo delle Terme. Rome.
Louvre. Paris.
Church of Saint Marie Saal, near Klagenfuirt.
Capitoline Museum. Rome.
Rome, speaking statue.
Restaurant, Via Adreatina. Rome.

BAS-RELIEFS

Vatican Museum. Rome.
Fragment of the Ara Pacis. Roman art of the first century B.C.
Fragment of a sarcophagus. Roman art. Louvre. Paris.
Sarcophagus. Greek art. Louvre. Paris.
Vatican Museum. Rome.
Vessel. Third or fourth century A.D. Museo Nazionale. Rome.
Detail of the great Cameo of the Sainte-Chapelle. Paris, Bibliotheque Nationale.
Cabinet des Medailles. Paris, Bibliotheque Nationale.

FRESCOES

The chapter head- and tailpieces are details of a ceiling from the Villa
Map of Germanicus' and Agrippina's voyage: Paul Jamotte
Decorative detail (third style). Pompeii.
Fresco from a house. Pompeii.
Fresco from the Farnesina. Museo delle Terme. Rome.
Painting from the Via Appia.
Detail of a fresco. Villa of Augustus. Rome.
Fresco from Herculaneum. Museo Nazionale. Naples.
Pompeian frescoes. Museo Nazionale. Naples.
Pompeian painting.
Frescoes from the Villa of Mysteries. Pompeii.

191

ACKNOWLEDGMENTS

Layout: Juliette Caputo

Sources: Françoise Borin

Map of Germanicus' and Agrippina's voyage: Paul Jamotte

Chris Marker (Editions du Seuil): pp. 4, 13, 33, 39, 40, 49, 57, 64, 77, 98, 100, 108, 144. Martine Wilmark Archives: pp. 27b, 27c, 27d, 136, 152. Anderson-Giraudon: 7 l., 10, 14, 16-17, 18, 55, 63 l. & r., 70, 75, 78-79, 89, 97, 105, 130, 163. Giraudon: pp. 7 r., 31, 34-35, 62 l. & r., 120-121, 128-129, 146, 154a, 154b, 155b, 159, 166, 167. Alinari-Giraudon: pp. 25, 43, 82, 85, 91, 92-93, 113. Bernand: pp. 174, 175. Roger Viollet: pp. 118, 155a. Archives La Minotaure: p. 27a. Institut d'Art et d'Archéologie (Editions du Seuil): pp. 46, 68, 74, 109, 111. Office du Tourisme Italien: p. 67. Cinémathèque: p. 86. Cahiers du Cinéma: p. 168.